D0319918

LIBRARIES NI
WITHDRAWN FROM STOCK

The **O** **G**rand **O**pera House Belfast

GRAND OPERA HOUSE

'A credit to our flourishing city'

Ulster Bank

The Grand Opera House Belfast

LYN GALLAGHER

NEELB LIBRARY AND INFORMATION CENTRE
DEMESNE AVENUE, BALLYMENA BT43 7BG

NUMBER   7036101

CLASS U/BEL-792-09

THE
BLACKSTAFF
PRESS

BELFAST

First published in 1995 by
The Blackstaff Press Limited
3 Galway Park, Dundonald, Belfast BT16 0AN, Northern Ireland
for the Grand Opera House
with the assistance of
the Ulster Bank Limited
and Belfast City Council

© Lyn Gallagher, 1995
All rights reserved

Typeset by Paragon Typesetters, Queensferry, Clwyd

Printed by W. & G. Baird Limited

A CIP catalogue record for this book
is available from the British Library

ISBN 0-85640-568-X

CONTENTS

FOREWORD

FOR THE GRAND OPERA HOUSE, the year 1995 is a special, almost astrological, conjunction – of age and youth, history and innovation, endurance and newness – and this book is published as part of its centenary celebrations.

Though it is the Grand Opera House's hundredth year, it is the Grand Opera House Trust's first. One year has passed since the newly formed Trust took over the reins of management of the theatre from the Arts Council of Northern Ireland. Over the century, the theatre had been run by a family business, by an entertainment corporation, by an arts council – but never before by a charitable trust.

The Trust was honoured to be invited to take responsibility for a building that is so closely associated with Belfast's history in the last hundred years. In 1895, when J.F. Warden opened his new theatre in Great Victoria Street, Belfast was a prosperous, confident city, and Frank Matcham reflected that confidence and sense of well-being in his bold, exuberant designs for the interior and the exterior. It is impossible to look at Matcham's auditorium, or at the Great Victoria Street frontage, without understanding the late Victorians' belief that their buildings – and the Opera House in particular – were built to endure.

And then, more recently, in the dark days of 1980, the restored and reopened Opera House was an affirmation of hope for a beleaguered city, a role, as fate would have it, that it was almost tragically to replay in 1991 and 1993. Despite it all it has endured to play its part in a new era in which confidence and prosperity are once more possible.

Now, the Trust has its mind and its sights on the next century, but to indicate that it has a proper respect for the past, it commissioned this book from Lyn Gallagher, with the brief that it should not be of interest only to historians of theatre, but also to the general reader, by reflecting the role the Grand Opera House has played in the life of Belfast and Northern Ireland generally. I am delighted with Lyn's success in accomplishing this.

The Grand Opera House has welcomed generations of Northern Ireland people, their faces briefly lit up by the reflected stage lights and the enlightenment of the events on the stage. This book brings those people back to life, glimpsed as inseparable partners of the actors, dancers, singers, and theatre staff. The Trust's pleasurable task is to keep the lights burning for the descendants of those past theatre-goers. I hope that, as you read it, you will share the Trust's delight in being part of what the Grand Opera House has stood for, and what it will stand for in its second century.

GEORGE PRIESTLEY OBE
CHAIRMAN, GRAND OPERA HOUSE TRUST

The New Grand Opera House
and Cirque, *c.* 1900
PUBLIC RECORD OFFICE OF
NORTHERN IRELAND

1

'A CREDIT TO
OUR FLOURISHING CITY'

T HE CURTAINS PARTED. The elegant Belfast audience – the leaders of the professions and commerce and their wives – sat in their comfortable seats and waited. It was a notable occasion, and all the dignitaries of civic and political life were present. The occupants of the stalls and the circle and the gallery marvelled at the decoration and luxury around them. They were privileged to be present, and they respected the expertise and sense of purpose of those who had brought this evening about.

There can have been little difference in the constitution of the audiences in 1895, when the Grand Opera House opened for the first time, and in 1980, when it enjoyed an equally glorious reopening. In the period that

Opposite:
The tiers of stage and circle
boxes; very little has changed
since they were designed and
constructed in 1895.
MONUMENTS AND BUILDINGS
RECORD

The White Star liner the *Georgic* was launched in 1895, the year the New Grand Opera House and Cirque was opened. The success of shipbuilders Harland and Wolff was one of the factors in the significant rise in Belfast's population.
ULSTER MUSEUM

J.F. Warden, proprietor of the New Grand Opera House and Cirque, which opened on 16 December 1895
PUBLIC RECORD OFFICE OF NORTHERN IRELAND

intervened, the theatre mirrored much of the life of the city it strove to delight or enlighten. It reflected the historical events of war and troubles, of prosperity and depression; it reflected the city's fashions, its tastes, its aspirations, but rarely its prejudices. On occasions the theatre and its audiences surpassed themselves: at other times they did not do themselves justice.

On the stage in front of the expectant house on 23 December 1895 before the commencement of the first performance stood two important and influential figures: J.F. Warden, the proprietor of the theatre, and Frank Matcham, the architect.

'Mr Matcham is father of more than forty theatres,' J.F. Warden announced. 'He has just told me of the particular affection he has for this, his youngest child.' If the remarkable theatre architect Frank Matcham could claim a position of paternal pride for Belfast's Grand Opera House, then he must share that pride with its owner, Warden, whose vigour, vision and acumen gave it birth, and who decided to build a theatre that would be 'a credit to our flourishing city'.

Joseph F. Warden was born in Hull on 12 December 1836, and from his first professional appearance at the age of eighteen on stage at Scarborough, his life revolved around the theatre. Success came early. In 1857, according to his obituary in the *Belfast News-Letter*, 'when Henry Irving was playing utility parts in Edinburgh, Mr Warden was in the lead at the Opera House in the same city'. Shortly afterwards he married Miss Jenny Bellairs, then principal comedienne with the Singing

Chambermaids, and together they travelled the British Isles in the tradition of the nineteenth-century theatre, spending a lengthy period in Dublin.

In 1863 Warden was appointed temporary manager of the Theatre Royal, Arthur Square, Belfast, and the following year the Theatre Royal reopened under the management of Messrs Warden and Mills. Although this began his enduring association with the city, Warden continued to visit London and the British provinces as an actor, taking many leading roles. He also made frequent appearances in Belfast and Ireland.

From 1870, however, his attention focused upon theatre management, and in particular the development of the Theatre Royal. He rebuilt the theatre in 1871, creating a grand establishment of polished stone, adorned by carvings of Shakespearean characters. Later in the decade, he turned his energy and enterprise to the northwest of Ulster, building the Opera House, Derry, as the *Belfast News-Letter* recorded:

> Stimulated by the appreciative manner in which the inhabitants of Derry had received his many efforts to amuse them, and perplexed by the insufficient accommodation afforded by the Corporation Hall for histrionic representation, Mr Warden resolved, early in 1877, to favour the Maiden City with an elaborate temple, dedicated solely to thespian pursuits. Mr Phipps, the eminent theatrical architect, was at once communicated with and as a consequence an admirable little structure, capable of holding 1,600 individuals, was erected in the Carlisle Road, and opened on Friday, 10th August, 1877.

J.F. Warden's energy and commitment to building was employed again in 1881 when the Theatre Royal burnt down. It was rebuilt and reopened within the year, on an even grander scale. Fourteen years later, the New Grand Opera House and Cirque, the only child of his building enterprise that survives today, was planned, and this time Warden approached the genius of Victorian theatre architecture, Frank Matcham.

Frank Matcham designed about 150 theatres throughout Britain, including many of the best-loved and most important theatres in the country. His work and contribution to the theatre is excellently documented in *Frank Matcham, Theatre Architect*, edited by Brian Walker. The Coliseum and the Palladium in London, the Opera House, Buxton, and the Gaiety Theatre at Douglas, on the Isle of Man, are a few examples of the opulent and practical buildings which gave Matcham an unrivalled reputation among his peers.

Matcham gained the friendship and esteem of the actors who played in his theatres. He had a particularly close friendship with Sir Henry Irving, who opened several of his theatres, and in his own right, he became a theatrical institution. When the Theatre Royal in Stockport opened, Jenny de Brent spoke the following lines before the curtain went up:

> In many houses drama finds a place:
> Ever the thousands of our English race
> Welcome the advent of we sons of art,
> Who show the passions of the human heart,

Frank Matcham, theatre architect, whose extravagant designs for the new opera house continue to please theatre goers today
GRAND OPERA HOUSE

As few the houses, reared with such Matchless skill,
As Matcham's work; his praise the world shall fill.

Lillie Langtry was equally enthusiastic but had to struggle with equally impossible scansion at the opening of the Cheltenham Theatre and Opera House:

Nay, where (within this house you'll all agree)
Not all can sit, but all can see –
The Architect's arrangements if you'll *watch 'em*
(Like these two rhymes), 'tis hard to *Match 'em*.'

By the middle of the present century, the extravagance of the decoration of Matcham's theatres no longer suited public taste, and his work became disregarded, but to the Belfast theatre-goers of 1895, the design of the New Grand Opera House and Cirque and decoration of the interior, described variously as 'exotic', 'continental', or 'Eastern', found few detractors. Indeed the journalists of 1895 struggled to describe adequately the wonders of the new theatre. The *Northern Whig* extolled the exterior:

The architect (Mr Frank Matcham of London) has succeeded in treating the elevations in a most artistic manner, the quaint gables, balustradings, minarets, etc, giving quite a continental appearance to the building; and the great width

The New Grand Opera House and Cirque, *c.* 1900
PUBLIC RECORD OFFICE OF NORTHERN IRELAND

of Glengall Place enables a capital view to be obtained of the whole. The Glengall Street front has an imposing central facade, flanked with square towers, crowned with boldly moulded and domed minarets, the centre portion having a richly designed pediment finished at the top with a carved finial from which an ornamental iron flambeau will cast a brilliant light at night, illuminating this and the adjoining streets. A large circular window lights the foyer over the entrance vestibule, and above this is a statue holding aloft an electric light.

The *Belfast News-Letter* entertained its readers with a vivid and minutely observed account of the richness of the interior:

> The ceiling is certainly novel and quite different in shape from what we have been used to. It is oblong across the auditorium with rounded corners and slightly coved, except the centre panel which is flat and contains a large sunlight only to be used in the case of the failure of electric light and for ventilating purposes. At the side drop handsome brass and copper electrioneers looped up at the centre. The large panel is filled in with a rich open work scrolled design and the outer core surrounding same has Indian scroll and strap work designs with large circular panels at the corners containing beautiful painted subjects representing the elements. The inner cove is painted to represent sky, with Indian palms and a balcony with vases and flowers and the whole when lighted by the electrioneers and the additional handsome drop lights has a most brilliant and charming Eastern effect.
>
> The ceiling is supported by Indian arches springing from the capitals of the columns, in which elephants' heads are introduced with quaint effect. The proscenium opening has a border of polished marble, surrounded with an enriched moulding with foliations and ornamental panelled corners, and over this there is a beautifully painted cartouche, with Indian figures representing music and dancing. On each side of the stage are two private boxes, between massive richly decorated columns. The fronts are boldly moulded and panelled and under the lower box is an arched entrance to the stalls. Over the top is a decorated minaret crowned with a half moon and crescent. At the side of this box facade are additional boxes on the grand circle level, divided by an arched panel from the entrance to the circle, which is designed as a facsimile of the boxes and has a very striking and withal cosy appearance.

Theatre-goers, who admired the decoration, may not have appreciated fully the innovative approach that Matcham had adopted to safety, both in the provision of sufficient exits and in complex fireproofing precautions, but they were sure to have enjoyed the benefits of his ventilation and of his faultless sightlines. The astute businessman in Warden doubtless valued Matcham's renowned ability to construct an elaborate building on a small site (which had been chosen for its excellent location), and to fill such a building with the maximum number of paying seats. Technically too, Matcham was a master of the staging required for a theatre that was expected to accommodate opera, variety and pantomime, as well as theatre of spectacular effect and, on occasion, the circus.

The traditions both of the circus and of transforming theatres into circuses were well established. Although circuses travelled from site to site,

Buff Bills / (LARRY PATTERSON) DIXIE GIRLS.
(THE FAMOUS
(IRISH CLOWN.)

Buffalo Bill's Dixie Girls and Larry Patterson, the famous Irish clown, part of a travelling circus, *c*. 1900
PUBLIC RECORD OFFICE OF NORTHERN IRELAND

very much as they do today, sometimes they would become resident, and Battye's Circus in Chichester Street was a substantial permanent establishment. As early as 1818, we hear that the Irish theatre entrepreneur Montagu Talbot 'has taken measures to convert all his theatres into such a disposition as will enable him to treat the towns in which they are with a troupe of excellent equestrians and pantomimers; the circus to open a few days after the theatre closes in each town'.

The prospectus for Warden Ltd highlights the desirable qualities of the New Grand Opera House and Cirque:

This house has been erected under the supervision of the eminent theatrical architect, Mr Frank Matcham, from plans prepared by him. The building is one of the finest and most extensive in the United Kingdom and it is estimated will accommodate 3,500. It is situated in one of the most central positions in Belfast, adjoining the terminus of the Great Northern Railway and the tramway cars pass the door from all parts of the city. . . . The bars have been let to a firm of high-class refreshment caterers. . . . By a simple mechanical contrivance . . . the theatre can within a few hours be converted into a grand circus. There is stabling for a large number of horses; and it will be obvious that this arrangement greatly enhances the value of the property.

The construction of the theatre is on the most approved design, and embraces the most recent improvements invented by Mr Matcham. There are separate exits from each part of the house, and there are no less than three wide exits from the pit alone. The entire building is fireproof so far as human ingenuity can make it so, and the stage is certainly separated from the auditorium by substantial walls and a fireproof asbestos curtain.

The proud owner and architect were no less effusive when they escorted a party of distinguished visitors prior to the unveiling of the memorial stone on 16 December 1895. They pointed out the modern devices by which, they claimed, the theatre could be emptied in three minutes: the special light-pressure automatic system of opening doors, and the novelty of tip-up seats. They demonstrated the capability of the proscenium arch to be made broader and higher for circuses, and the ability, by mechanical screw gearing, to lower the stage completely, thereby achieving a suitable circus arena, and they ensured that no detail designed for decoration, comfort, or enchantment escaped the attention of the party.

Nearly a century later, in 1980, John Earl, then the surveyor of the Greater London Council's Historic Buildings Division, assessed the architect's celebrated talent to marry the decorative and the practical. 'It is worth underlining the fact that his theatres were as near to being *functionally* perfect as limitations of site and budget would permit. His ravishing decorative schemes did not, indeed, look forward to the shuttered concrete audience-containers of today, nor were they as self-consciously high-minded as, say, Verity's Scala, but they, too, fulfilled a function which was regarded at the time as being essential. The theatre auditorium was designed to produce an atmosphere of opulent comfort and to excite expectancy. Its decoration seduced the eye in the full light before the curtain rose, and looked rich and mysterious with the house lights down. The theatre was an exciting place to be in. The theatre architect was concerned not merely with serviceability and safety, but also with enchantment. Not only "commoditie and firmnesse" but also "delight".'

Warden's acumen and ambition in commissioning Matcham for his new enterprise reflected a confidence in his own business ability, an ability which was in turn valued by the Belfast public. J.F. Warden seems to have risen above Belfast society's innate suspicion of things theatrical. He built a fine house in 1891 in Adelaide Park, which he appropriately christened Shakespeare House, and the impression given by this suburban villa by the architect James J. Phillips is one of substantial respectability, with the only concession to extravagance in the highly ornamental cast-iron balustrading and veranda. During his career he seems to have won the affection as well as the respect of his fellow citizens, and at a benefit night 'the pleasing testimonial of esteemed theatrical friends and general public of Belfast' resulted in the presentation of a purse of 700 guineas to himself and a diamond

Late-Victorian theatres were technically well equipped. This prompt corner with electric lighting board was photographed in the Theatre Royal, Birmingham, shortly before its demolition in 1901.
BIRMINGHAM LIBRARY SERVICES

bracelet for his wife. His status was reflected in the fact that during his last illness he was attended by the prominent local physicians Doctors Whitla and O'Connell, and finally Professor Sinclair. The extremely warm *Belfast News-Letter* obituary describes the 'genial JF' as one who 'knew all the aspects of the stage – its seamy aspect as well as its brighter – but it never embittered his disposition'. It sums him up as 'a Bohemian but of high class . . . an actor first, kind-hearted man second, keen business man third'.

The great Shakespearean actor Frank Benson as Shylock; at the opening ceremony for the New Grand Opera House and Cirque on 16 December 1895 Benson unveiled a memorial tablet.
THEATRE MUSEUM, V. & A.

That his contacts within the theatrical world were of the first order is evidenced by the quality of performers whom he persuaded to come to Belfast. Sarah Bernhardt had played at the Theatre Royal in 1881, and in the same year, while the theatre was being rebuilt, Warden brought Henry Irving and Ellen Terry to the Ulster Hall. The renowned Shakespearean actor Frank Benson, a great Belfast favourite, recalled that 'to those who were admitted to Mr Warden's private confidence and friendship, he was a most charming companion. His recollections, stories, his keen shrewd wit and caustic satire were things to be heard.'

One story that has been cited as an illustration of Warden as 'actor first, kind-hearted man second' concerns a visit to Manchester, where he ran into a miserable young man confounded by stage fright. He was due to appear as Iago in *Othello* in an amateur production, before an audience he needed to impress, and he was extremely uncertain of his ability to do so. Warden offered to exchange places with him, his repertoire of Shakespearean roles causing him no difficulty in this last-minute understudy role, and won for the young man tumultuous applause. No doubt Warden himself enjoyed the unexpected limelight.

Warden's description as 'keen business man' is equally justified, and his own dealings with the Grand Opera House, until his death in 1898, were characterised by a clever business approach. The *Belfast News-Letter* noted with approval that, 'So sanguine was Mr Warden in the success of the venture that he deposited sufficient money in the bank to ensure the share holders of their dividend, whether the theatre was a success or not.' The first directors of the new limited liability company of Warden Ltd were J.F. Warden, W.J. Jury (founder of the Dublin hotel), S.C. Allen (a Belfast printer), and H.H. Morell (joint manager of the Haymarket Theatre, and lessee of the Shaftesbury Avenue Theatre in London).

Warden ensured that the building of the Grand Opera House was completed as speedily as the rebuilding of the Theatre Royal in 1881. The plans were submitted to Belfast Corporation in November 1894, and the whole contract was carried out by the main contractors, H. & J. Martin, with numerous specialist subcontractors, within twelve months.

The choice of site was a good one from a business point of view, as the

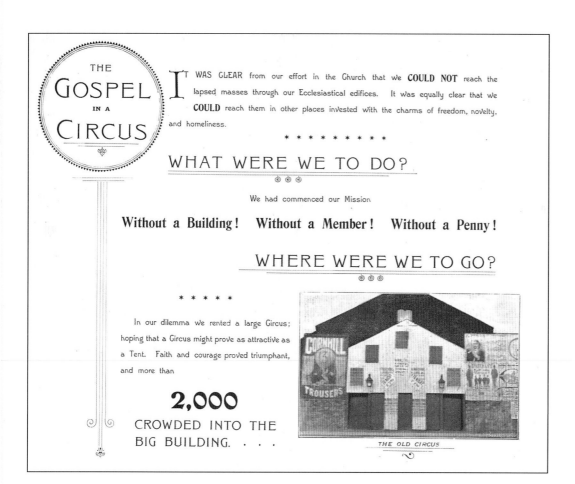

THE GOSPEL IN A CIRCUS

IT WAS CLEAR from our effort in the Church that we COULD NOT reach the lapsed masses through our Ecclesiastical edifices. It was equally clear that we COULD reach them in other places invested with the charms of freedom, novelty, and homeliness.

* * * * * * * * *

WHAT WERE WE TO DO?

We had commenced our Mission

Without a Building!   Without a Member!   Without a Penny!

WHERE WERE WE TO GO?

* * * * *

In our dilemma we rented a large Circus; hoping that a Circus might prove as attractive as a Tent. Faith and courage proved triumphant, and more than

2,000 CROWDED INTO THE BIG BUILDING. . . .

THE OLD CIRCUS

prospectus for Warden Ltd had made clear. Access to public transport was its most attractive quality. Belfast people were already used to enjoying evening excursions to the centre of the town for entertainment, and as early as the 1860s the Theatre Royal had been advertising the availability of special late trains, run by Northern Counties, which departed at 11.30 for Carrickfergus, Sydenham and Bangor. The site also had the advantage of having been for some time a destination for people in search of entertainment. The Grand Opera House was built on the site of Ginnet's Circus, which, when it opened in November 1882, had itself been seen as a welcome addition to the recreational opportunities provided in Belfast. The *Belfast Evening Telegraph* had shared in the general enthusiasm:

> This magnificent new circus will undoubtedly supply a want long felt by the public of Belfast and be the means of providing an innocent and thoroughly enjoyable entertainment for many thousands who, heretofore, have vainly longed for some place in which they could shake off the worry and care of the day's business and recuperate their energies by healthy relaxation.

The circus boasted a promenade, pit and gallery, and lighting 'on an entirely new principle' with numerous handsomely mounted gasoliers. During its short history it featured a military tournament staged by one Robert Baden-Powell, a captain of the Fifth Dragoon Guards, later to become the founder of the Boy Scout movement.

Ginnet's Circus stood on the site of the New Grand Opera House and Cirque in Glengall Street. The building was used by the Methodist Belfast Central Mission for services before it found a permanent home in the Grosvenor Hall.
BELFAST CENTRAL MISSION

In 1889, Dr R. Crawford Johnson, who had had a most successful summer tent mission in nearby Hunter Street, looked to the owner of Ginnet's to house his Methodist church services when winter came. Mr Ginnet agreed to let the premises, on condition that the religious services were of a respectable nature and that the rent was paid in advance. From these services sprang the congregation that built the Grosvenor Hall. It is a strange coincidence that in the New Grand Opera House and Cirque seven years later, the founder of the Salvation Army, General William Booth, preached to full houses three times in one day, the first and possibly the last time the theatre had been used for divine worship. This system of hiring a theatre for such a purpose, although apparently common in England, was considered novel in Belfast. The services were simple and direct, and the general, while a little disappointing as an elocutionist, was thought to be an impressive and earnest preacher.

Warden began his new enterprise knowing that there was substantial demand for popular entertainment in the city, and believing that his audience was ready for a wider dramatic repertoire. The population of Belfast was rising rapidly: it was to increase from 90,000 in 1850 to 350,000 in 1901. As the twelfth-largest city in the United Kingdom, it was bigger than Dublin, and Warden felt justified in thinking that the patronage of its citizens would sustain another theatre, and that the Grand Opera House and Theatre Royal could complement each other. His prospectus stresses this:

It has been found on very many occasions that the present Theatre Royal has been inadequate for certain large-scale productions, and also to accommodate the numbers who sought to gain admission, and hence the building of the new Grand Opera House, which will likewise provide a first-class circus at other times of the year. It is intended as far as possible to vary the class of entertainment presented at the same time at each Theatre. Many English towns with considerably less population than Belfast can support two and even three theatres, and when it is borne in mind that the population of Belfast (which now stands about 300,000) is increasing, according to the last census, at the rate of 5,000 per annum, it cannot be doubted that a large measure of success will attend the undertaking.

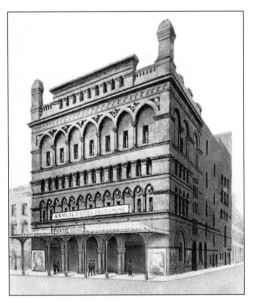

The Theatre Royal, Arthur Square, which was owned by the proprietor of the New Grand Opera House and Cirque, J.F. Warden
GRAND OPERA HOUSE

The population of Belfast had certainly already been enjoying a great variety of entertainment. The Theatre Royal had continued to produce popular and classical drama, with a strong 'stock' or repertory cast and distinguished visiting actors, maintaining a tradition that had begun vigorously in the eighteenth century. In the last quarter of that century two theatres had flourished in the town – the Vaults theatre in Ann Street and another at Mill Gate – and Sarah Siddons visited to an enthusiastic reception. Historian George Benn, writing in 1823, states, 'There is likewise a theatre in Belfast, very excellently and tastefully fitted up in the inside, though its exterior is not only unornamental, but heavy and disagreeable.' But as the nineteenth century progressed, the theatre waned. Gradually, the influx of great numbers into the town and the popularisation of entertainment led to a distancing of the gentry from the theatre, and when Thackeray visited Belfast in 1842 he was surprised that his gentleman host had 'never been in the playhouse, and never heard of anyone going there'. Thackeray found a sparsely filled pit, but a gallery 'quite full, and exceedingly happy and noisy'. The scandal of a murder perpetrated after a drunken night at the theatre led to a campaign of opprobrium by the churches in 1844, and a reduction in patronage by respectable citizens, with a subsequent reduction in the quality of the shows. By the 1850s one theatre was presenting five acts of *Julius Caesar*, including some dancing by Madame Angelique and songs by the Irish tenor Mr Ryan, followed by a farce, while an advertisement of the same time contained this announcement:

> Production of a Grand Oriental Spectacle, with New Scenery, Correct Costumes, Extensive Platforms, Terrific Combats, Imposing Marches, Striking Tableaux, etc., illustrating the celebrated picture of Belshazzar's Feast and the meeting of Cleopatra and Antony on the banks of the Nile. In this Gorgeous Phantasy entitled 'The Siege of Jerusalem' with its Egyptian Ballet, there will be engaged the Whole Strength of the Company and Numerous Auxiliaries.

An account of audience behaviour at Sadler's Wells in the 1850s gives some idea of how theatre audiences of the time might behave:

> The play was *Macbeth*. It was performed amidst the usual hideous medley of fights, foul language, catcalls, shrieks, yells, oaths, blasphemy, obscenity, apples, oranges, nuts, biscuits, ginger beer, porter and pipes – not that there was any particular objection to the Play, but that the audience were, on the whole, in a condition of mind, generally requiring such utterance. Pipes of all lengths were at work in the gallery; several were displayed in the pit. Cans of beer, each with a pint measure to drink from (for the convenience of gentlemen who had neglected the precaution of bringing their own pots in their bundles), were carried through the dense crowd at all stages of the tragedy. Sickly children in arms were squeezed out of shape, in all parts of the house. Fish was fried at the entrance doors. Barricades of oyster-shells encumbered the pavement. Expectant half-price visitors to the gallery howled defiant impatience up the stairs, and danced a sort of Carmagnole all round the building.

In the same decade the Theatre Royal in Belfast had put on a play called *The Hypocrite*. This was seen in certain quarters as a lampoon on religion, and a prolonged and effective attack on the theatre was sustained under the able leadership of the Reverend Doctor Henry Cooke, the famous 'Black Man' of the statue at College Square. Many Protestant congregations of Belfast were urged, week after week, to spurn the evil of theatres. Although when Warden took over the Theatre Royal in 1863 the effects of this attack on the theatre had been mitigated significantly, a climate of moral censure persisted and in 1881 led to the shunning of Sarah Bernhardt because the French play she was due to appear in was not considered to be quite proper.

BELFAST CENTRAL LIBRARY

Impropriety abounded, however, in the flourishing singing saloons and music-halls of the city. The Alhambra led the field until the Empire Theatre of Varieties in Victoria Square was established in 1894. John Gray, in *Belfast: the Making of a City*, notes a significant change in the pattern of the audiences:

> The Empire attracted an entirely new audience. For the first time women could attend without fear of reproach, and the lavish interior overcame the qualms of the business classes. At the same time the Empire directly threatened the working-class audience of the Alhambra, which now found it difficult to attract the best artistes because the variety chains, including the Empire, were signing them up on exclusive contracts.

Gray adds that the showing of the first cinematographs at the Empire and the Alhambra was 'symptomatic of the rapid changes in the organisation and technology of entertainment towards the end of the century'.

Between the theatre and the music-hall sat the pantomime. Perennially popular, by 1895 it had grown out of all recognition from the harlequinade mime show of the early century into a spectacular creation that was to change very little in the century that followed. A box office certainty, it won the favour of audiences across the divide of class.

More respectable entertainments were creeping onto the social agenda of Belfast. At the Victoria Music Hall in May Street, where Charles Dickens gave a reading in 1858, lectures and concerts were interspersed with presentations by the Pickwick Dramatic Club, that included drama and farce. Regular 'literary and musical melanges' featured elocutionists, ventriloquists and 'character delineations'. The Belfast Philharmonic Society had been formed from two amateur societies, the Classical Harmonists and the Anacreontic, in 1874, and amateur operatic companies had begun to win converts. The Ulster Hall, when it was opened in 1862, was one of the largest halls of its type in the United Kingdom, capable of holding an audience of 2,000. It housed drama and concerts of classical music including the obligatory renderings of the *Messiah*. Occasionally the programme veered in the direction of novelty, as in 1892 when a concert of classical music included La Belle Siffleuse, an American lady whistler.

In marked contrast to respectable Belfast's attitude towards theatre was its unqualified enthusiasm for opera, and the productions of the Royal Carl Rosa Opera Company at the Theatre Royal were well attended, especially by the upper strata of the city's society, who saw the visit of the opera as a fashionable highlight.

So, at the same time as the unsophisticated taste of the new working classes of Belfast was creating a demand for a certain type of entertainment, there were optimistic signs of cultural reawakening which must have given Warden grounds for hope that more drama of a more serious kind would be welcome and well supported. In addition, there were tangible signs that Belfast's cultural identity was growing stronger. In 1890, the formation of the Belfast Art Society had laid the foundations for the body that would eventually become the Royal Ulster Academy of Arts. In the same year, the Belfast Free Public Library, Art Gallery and Museum opened, and a year later the Kit Kat Club, a literary association of poets, was founded.

John Gray sees the emergence of the Grand Opera House as the natural conclusion of the changes that had taken place in the nineteenth century.

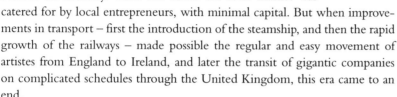

LINEN HALL LIBRARY

> The arrival of the Grand Opera House, in 1895, which presented the best of English artistes and productions, confirmed the theatre's return to respectability, after a century of chequered fortune. . . . Rising incomes and particularly the emergence of a skilled working class, a very marked feature of Belfast society, created new possibilities and entertainment became an industry. Until the 1870s the local market was catered for by local entrepreneurs, with minimal capital. But when improvements in transport – first the introduction of the steamship, and then the rapid growth of the railways – made possible the regular and easy movement of artistes from England to Ireland, and later the transit of gigantic companies on complicated schedules through the United Kingdom, this era came to an end.
>
> The full flowering of this uni-cultural merry-go-round could not occur until local entrepreneurs had developed their market to a point which enabled them to provide the touring companies with the appropriate facilities. In Belfast this progression occurred well within the working lives of the first generation of substantial entrepreneurs. Its main requirement was a large audience, and both in the theatre and elsewhere this helped to dictate the nature of the entertainment, with an emphasis on blandness rather than bawdiness, and the use of entertainments which had proved successful elsewhere rather than local experiment.

Warden knew that he had in the Grand Opera House a theatre that could handle any show in the spectrum of late-Victorian entertainment, from circus to Shakespeare. He must also have felt gratified by the huge fund of goodwill that existed towards himself and the new theatre, when he read, before the theatre had even opened its doors, the following effusive newspaper report, evoking the great theatrical tradition flowing from the sixth-century-BC poet Thespis, held to be the founder of drama:

> The presiding genius of ancient drama in our city (Mr J.F. Warden) has well won the congratulations and best wishes of its many devotees for the remarkable enterprise displayed by him in catering for their fastidious tastes. He has not to no purpose recognised the enormous strides made by the commercial capital of the Emerald Isle and not being content with bringing the cream of the dramatic profession to our favourite house in Arthur Square, he with laudatory zeal and commendable enterprise commenced the erection of a new Grand Opera House, which the patronage of the other temple of Thespis amply justified. This last act of Mr Warden's will endear him more than ever to the Belfast public. . . . Mr Warden is known to all, and even the very children recall his name with more than ordinary pleasure as they

remember that it is at the waving of his wand that those marvellous constructions of wonder and delight known as Pantomime are laid before their eyes. Mr Warden's efforts to supply good, wholesome entertainments for the public have been appreciated. . . . Belfast has often been the deserved, or undeserved recipient of hard hits on the score of its sober-headed and non-musical character, its inhabitants supposed to be so much engrossed with their commercial pursuits in their desire to make money – and that rapidly – that they have no time to devote to the high arts. While this was not altogether the case, it is gratifying to find that with its increasing opulence a change for the better has come.

After thirty years in the theatre in Belfast, Warden would have been confident in his knowledge of his audience, so it was quite natural that a week after the theatre was formally opened by Frank Benson, it opened its doors to pantomime.

'Our Theatrical Warden';
Fred Warden succeeded his father, J.F.
Warden, as manager of the New Grand
Opera House and Cirque in 1898.
MAGPIE

NEW

Grand Opera House

Great Victoria Street,
Belfast.

AND CIRQUE.

Great Victoria Street,
Belfast.

Proprietors, ... "WARDEN, LIMITED." | Managing Director, ... Mr. J. F. WARDEN.
Business Manager, ... Mr. Fred W. Warden. | Secretary, ... Mr. A. A. Macaulay.

MR. WARDEN begs to announce that the above Magnificent Building will

OPEN TO THE PUBLIC

MONDAY, December 23rd next

ONE OF THE MOST BEAUTIFUL AND SUBSTANTIAL STRUCTURES IN THE THREE KINGDOMS,

FRANK MATCHAM, Architect, London.
H. & J. MARTIN, Contractors, Belfast.

GRAND OPERA HOUSE

2
SUCCESS AND CIRCUSES

WITH A CHARACTERISTIC EYE FOR PUBLICITY J.F. Warden formally opened the New Grand Opera House and Cirque a week before the pantomime was to start. Just as he must have expected, the newspapers gave the event maximum coverage. As well as the rapturous descriptions of the theatre itself, the unveiling of the memorial tablet, which has now disappeared, was fully reported. The unveiling by Frank Benson took place at 6.30 p.m., 16 December 1895, after a tour of the theatre by the dignitaries present. Mr G.W. Wolff MP (the Wolff of Harland & Wolff, who had become MP for East Belfast in 1892)

Lettering from the first New Grand Opera House and Cirque programme cover before 1900
GRAND OPERA HOUSE

moved that Captain James McCalmont MP should be chairman, and in his speech, McCalmont stressed Belfast's record of affection for the stage, and with complimentary reference to the wonders of the modern conveniences of the Grand Opera House he recalled that it was not so long ago that stage lighting was effected by candles, which were then superseded by pans of oil in which a wick floated. Now every theatre had a limelight man instead of a candle woman, McCalmont observed.

McCalmont then introduced Frank Benson, who explained that he had travelled to Belfast from London on his way to Newcastle upon Tyne, where he would lay a foundation stone for another new theatre the next day. He expressed his pleasure at receiving the invitation from 'one whom they all respected and honoured' – Mr J.F. Warden – who 'had never lost his knowledge or his love for the art for which he had been in his time a distinguished ornament'. Benson continued with felicitous remarks about Belfast, 'where the love of theatre is so strong', and according to one newspaper report told his select audience that

> the art which he had the honour to belong to was essentially, he thought, an Irish art. At least it was an art which seemed to him to appeal to an extraordinary extent to Irishmen and Irishwomen, and it was an art which a greater number of Irishmen and Irishwomen had adorned than almost any other section of the British community.

He finished with the happy thought that though the house was empty now, it might be the last empty house in the theatre's history.

The event finished with the presentation by Warden to Frank Benson of a breast pin of the head of Shakespeare which Warden had been given by the celebrated tragedian William Charles Macready. With suitable dramatic impact he explained that it had been given to him with the words, 'I have worn this for a number of years; take it, my boy, and wear it for my sake, until you see and know someone you would like to give it to who would wear it for the sake of the old tragedian.'

A week later, on Monday, 23 December, the New Grand Opera House and Cirque flung back its doors for a gala opening performance. After the overture was played, 'God Save the Queen' was sung by the entire company and audience and the theatre was declared open by Lord Arthur Hill MP. Speaking from the Royal Box, he said how pleased he was to be present on this momentous occasion in the theatrical history of Belfast. He was seconded by Captain McCalmont. Warden then took the stage to read out telegrams of congratulations from theatre managers from all over the British Isles, and in his turn introduced the architect, Frank Matcham.

As well as the qualities of the 'original, farcical, comical, funny, pantomime "Blue Beard", or "Is Marriage a Failure?" ', the programme gives all the practical details required by the potential audience. An important notice assures patrons that no tramcars will be withdrawn from Great Victoria Street before 7.30 p.m., and that late cars will pass the theatre for Balmoral, Windsor, Botanic Gardens, Sandy Row Junction, Crumlin

Road, Shankill Road, Connswater and Sydenham, Antrim Road, Falls Road and Mountpottinger.

For the patrons of the best seats, however, a system was available by which the carriages of the wealthy would line up in Glengall Street. Each carriage was allocated a number when it arrived and after the show a man would stand outside at the front of the theatre and call out the numbers for the coachmen, who would then in turn pull out of the line and come and pick up their passengers.

The first programme for the new theatre also lays out very clearly the prices of admission and the different entrances for admission (which separated patrons for each section, and therefore kept the classes distinct), the special arrangements for children (half-price but children-in-arms not admitted), and the method of 'securing' seats at no extra charge by applying to the box office daily from 10 a.m. to 3 p.m. Prices ranged from 4s. for the dress circle to 6d. for the gallery. Boxes were charged at 20s. to 40s. At this time labourers earned 16s. to 19s. per week, with tradesmen receiving twice that sum. 'Early' tickets were available for a supplement. Purchasers of early tickets were more sure of their seats (although they ran the risk of a crush at the door) and often enjoyed the sometimes uproarious conduct of their fellows in the gods in spontaneous 'warm-up' sessions during the time before the curtain rose. It was a custom that persisted into the middle of the twentieth century.

The resident orchestra of the Grand Opera House, under its musical director, Edgar Haines, played almost continuously, and the pantomime included the Primrose Ballet Troupe under ballet mistress Madame Eugenie. The audiences of Belfast were to be denied no opportunity of seeing *Blue Beard*. Performances went on throughout Christmas, with 'Three Grand Morning Performances' on 25, 26 and 27 December at 1.30 p.m.

Edgar Haines, the 'leader' of the resident orchestra of the New Grand Opera House and Cirque, 1899
MAGPIE

As the season started, every programme, price one penny, contained the 'Important Notice' that the saloons of the theatre would serve tea, coffee, sandwiches, confectionery and fruit, and that wines, spirits, liquors, stout, beer and mineral water, cigars and cigarettes of the best brands only would be available. The owner of the franchise was the company P. & F. McGlade, proprietors of bars and billiard halls throughout the city, who in the 1990s were still operating in Donegall Street. The theatre programmes were elegant in design, and unapologetically aimed towards the respectable of Belfast society. A mature lady in evening dress stands at the foot of the curve of an imposing staircase, conversing with a young and sophisticated pair, while other, equally well-dressed patrons sweep upwards, towards the delights of the dress circle. The programmes were well supported with advertisements, many appropriate to the theatre, such as those for opera glasses. Others, such as the advertisements for electric light installation, took full advantage of the fact that the audience was enjoying the novelty of a generously lit theatre.

With all the commercial aspects of his business in hand, Warden

GRAND OPERA HOUSE

GRAND OPERA HOUSE

played fairly safe with his choice of shows for his first season. The bill of fare concentrated on popular entertainment. He presented *Eve Up-to-date, an Adamless Eden*, described as a burlesque, *All Aboard* and *The French Maid*, which were musical comedies, *The Shop Girl* (twice in the first year), which was hailed as the 'greatest musical farce of recent times', *The Old Toll House*, a 'melodrama of the customary type', *The Lady Slavey*, a 'highly successful go-as-you-please Musical Piece', and (a dip towards melodrama) *Swiss Express*, which promised comedians and 'Pantomimists', with 'high kickers from Paris'.

A production of *My Girl*, a 'domestic musical play' which included a bicycle dance, drew special attention because Warden's younger son, John, appeared in it as the Hebrew. The *Belfast News-Letter* thoroughly approved:

> On coming before the assemblage that filled the Grand Opera House from top to bottom, Mr John A. Warden met with a welcome that had all the warmth of an ovation. He proved that on the ground of merit alone, to say nothing of the long association, he was well worthy of it. Mr Warden is a true humorist, with the prospect of a brilliant future before him. He has gained immensely in power, depth and expression since he was last upon the local stage.

The George Edwardes Company specialised in the best-selling musical comedies of the London stage. Shows such as *The Circus Girl* and *The Runaway Girl* were easy sellers and returned often. When one of the most popular musical plays, *The Geisha*, was presented, advertisements promised that the Grand Opera House would be turned into a garden of flowers, and that 'This theatre will be perfumed every performance of this engagement with the "Geisha Perfume" (the most delicious perfume extant) by W.A. LYNASS, the Store Chemist, 5 Ann Street. Free samples will be distributed.' Another company which specialised in popular musicals was that belonging to Mr Morell and Mr Mouillot, whose *A Greek Slave* was a box office success throughout the country.

Sometimes a visiting play would encourage a new type of audience, but this was not always to the taste of one local theatre critic:

The Morell–Mouillot company toured the British Isles with popular musicals and plays; they brought *A Greek Slave* to Belfast in 1898.
THEATRE MUSEUM, V. & A.

> *The Football King* is, as its name suggests, a play in which the associations of the winter pastime constitute the principal interest; and it was evident by the character of the audience assembled in the Grand Opera House last evening and in the reception of the production that that appeal is not made in vain to the sympathies of the football loving section of the public. To the ordinary playgoer the piece is one which makes an enormous draught upon the imagination.

Some straightforward drama was included. The Adelphi Theatre Company brought plays that were neither musical nor comic, such as *The Harbour Lights*, but for lovers of classical drama the highlight was the visit of Frank Benson and his Shakespearean Company every New Year. With breathtaking versatility, and presumably interchangeable scenery, these travelling companies were able to present up to ten different productions in a visit. In February 1896, Benson's company put on *Hamlet*, *Romeo and Juliet*, *Othello*, *The Taming of the Shrew*, *The Merchant of Venice*, and *As You Like It*; such was the popularity of the actor that full houses were assured. There existed a bond between Benson and the Belfast audiences that other famous actors did not succeed in establishing. Warden brought him on succeeding years to appear immediately after the pantomime run ended, a juxtaposition that the *Belfast News-Letter* remarked upon on 26 January 1897:

> From Pantomime to Shakespearian drama is a violent transition; and last night, when the streets lay white with snow, was most Christmaslike, and 'Little Bo-Peep' and the harlequinade would have been in keeping with the weather. But Benson was here; and the Belfast public, being fond of Benson, would not be deterred either by sentimental considerations or those of weather from seeing their favourite. So they foregathered at the 'Grand' in large numbers, every section in the well-filled pit, gallery, and circle; and the plaudits which re-echoed again and again through the lofty auditorium testified anew to the warm place which Mr Benson occupies in the heart of the Belfast public, and to the unbounded delight with which they hail his annual appearance among them.

Benson played Romeo to Mrs Constance Benson's Juliet, Othello to her Desdemona, and with Mrs Benson as Ophelia he gave a Hamlet, which one critic said 'shows more study and inspiration every year'. For *The Rivals*, the Grand Opera House was filled from pit to gallery, and Benson's Captain Absolute showed 'in the most agreeable manner a talent for humorous impersonation but rarely met with in a professed exponent of tragedy'. In the audience were the lord mayor and lady mayoress, and a large body of Queen's College students. In his closing remarks Benson stated that it gave him 'the greatest pleasure to contribute to the amusement of the great population of the industrious city of Belfast. He believed that in a community such as this, where the brain was so closely and so continuously kept at work, occasional recreation was required.' Benson did credit to the cerebral capacity of his Grand Opera House audiences by bringing *Richard II*, a courageous revival of an unpopular play that was and is very rarely performed. His general contribution to the world of the theatre was enormous, and it is widely accepted that the grounding and education he was able to give to talented young actors of the day was fundamental to the theatre of the time.

Sir John Gielgud remembered watching Frank Benson's company when he was about eight years old.

> The first Shakespeare play I ever saw was *As You Like It* at the Coronet Theatre, Notting Hill Gate, with Benson and Dorothy Green. This must have been in about 1912 or 1913. Of course I only took in the plot and the scenery. There was solid ivy for Orlando to nail on to a very shaky canvas wall in the opening scene, and the terraces of Duke Frederick's garden were ingeniously transformed into forest glades by covering them with autumn leaves, which the actors had to plough through for the rest of the performance.

Frank Benson, whose Shakespearean Company were regular visitors to Belfast from 1896 to 1931
GRAND OPERA HOUSE

Richard D'Oyly Carte, whose opera company came to the New Grand Opera House and Cirque from its earliest years
THEATRE MUSEUM, V. & A.

THEATRE MUSEUM, V. & A.

A few years later Gielgud vividly remembered an occasion when he sat in the upper circle of Drury Lane Theatre on 2 May 1916. *Julius Caesar* was being performed for a Shakespeare Tercentenary Performance before King George and Queen Mary, arranged by Sir George Alexander.

> During one of the intervals, we hear a great outburst of cheering from behind the curtain, and someone comes out to tell us that Frank Benson, who is playing Caesar, has just been sent for to the Royal Box, still in his corpse-like make-up as the ghost, to be knighted by the King with a sword hastily borrowed from Simmonds, the theatrical costumier's round the corner in King Street. The audience cheer wildly at the announcement, taking up the applause from the huge crowd of delighted players behind the scenes.

Warden opened the doors of his prestigious new theatre not only to professional entertainers but also to the amateur operatic companies of the city, whilst the D'Oyly Carte Opera Company came regularly and were always well received. A sure crowd-puller was the annual visit of the Royal Carl Rosa Opera Company. They presented a range of operas that would be unthinkable today, and they featured a repertoire in which Wagner was always included. Mozart made a very rare appearance. Belfast audiences in the first season of the Grand Opera House saw *Carmen*, *Cavalleria rusticana*, *I Pagliacci*, *Mignon*, *Tannhäuser*, *The Flying Dutchman* and *The Mastersingers*, and supported the visit well, so that when anticipating their 1897 tour, the writer in the *Belfast News-Letter* was able to state:

> The visit of the Carl Rosa Opera Company is an event much looked forward to in Belfast Musical circles, and the opening performance last evening was well worthy of the best traditions of a company that has done so much to forward operatic music in the kingdom. The opera given was *Tannhäuser* and it was received with tremendous enthusiasm by one of the most appreciative audiences that ever graced the interior of the Grand Opera House. This is a significant fact in itself, and shows in what direction the musical taste of the city is tending. Belfast sees so little of grand opera that a visit such as the one in question comes as a boon and a blessing. A matter for regret – and this has always been the keynote of local critics' complaints – is the comparatively short stay of the Carl Rosa. The musical progress of the city is a fact too evident to be argued and there is surely enough musical enthusiasm to ensure a longer visit than has heretofore been the case. Judging from last year's audiences there is no question but that it would pay all the parties well.

The writer added that Belfast audiences that year would be treated to two Wagnerian performances – and to a new opera, *La Bohème*, by 'a promising young Italian named Puccini'.

Given that the first performance of this opera had been at Turin in the previous year, and that London had not seen the opera, the conservative taste of the Belfast audience was to be tested, and it was with some satisfaction that the *Belfast News-Letter* entered into the traditional rivalry between Dublin and Belfast in the field of artistic preference.

Notwithstanding the cold and cynical attitude of the Dublin audience, Belfast received Puccini's new opera *La Bohème* literally with open arms, and with a degree of enthusiasm that would be hard to beat. The Grand Opera House was well filled and the farthest expectations of the work which had been formed by many were more than amply justified.

The writer Forrest Reid was to champion the cause of opera in Belfast in the next decade. As a young man he experienced the packed, enthusiastic houses that greeted the visits of the Royal Carl Rosa Opera Company, and something of the flavour of a Belfast night at the opera is recorded in his novel *Peter Waring*:

'Would you like to come with me to the opera to-night?' he whispered to me one morning.

We were seated together on the window-sill in Doctor Gwynn's classroom, sharing a much bescribbled *Virgil*. We always sat there, a little aloof from the rest of the class, and as the doctor was very old, blind, and rather deaf, it was possible to pass the time quite pleasantly without attracting his attention.

I had not yet been inside a theatre, and had never even thought of going to one, but the suggestion was thrilling. 'What opera is it?' I asked.

'*Faust*,' he whispered, 'Gounod's *Faust*. . . . If you come I'll meet you outside the theatre at a quarter to seven.'

'Very well: I'll be there.'

He told me more about it later, but not very much, as he had never been to an opera himself. . . . We had arrived too soon − even for the early door, for which you paid sixpence extra . . . two long queues by now stretched from the pit and gallery entrances. Presently the doors were opened, and slowly we squeezed our way in. The stalls were still nearly empty, but the pit was soon crowded, and I gazed round me with the liveliest interest. In another quarter of an hour the stalls too began to fill up.

The fireproof curtain was lowered and raised − just to show that it worked . . . the orchestra straggled in and began to tune their fiddles. Then, after a due pause, the conductor followed, a fat little German with a bald domed head which glimmered palely, like an ostrich's egg. He faced the audience, bowed two or three times to their applause, and finally, turning round, tapped the music-stand sharply with his baton. He raised both hands, and the first phrase was drawn out slowly on the strings.

Somehow it was a wonderful moment − all that was to come being still so excitingly uncertain. With the end of the overture the lights were lowered, and the curtain rose on the lonely Faust, seated in his study at a table, upon which were a skull, an hour-glass, and a large open book. . . . I was surprised to find that this old grey-bearded man, who resembled in the distance an Albert Dürer print, had a fresh tenor voice. Outside his window, and invisible to us, some peasants were singing as they passed. Faust heard them also, and their chant seemed to fill him with despair. Suddenly, in a light of red flame, Mephistopheles appeared. Faust pleaded passionately for his lost youth, and Mephistopheles offered to restore it − at a price. Then, miraculously, the wall of the room dissolved like a mist, and a magic vision of Margaret, seated at her spinning wheel, took shape before us, while the swinging sensual phrase of temptation, repeated again and again in the orchestra, lulled me to a dreamy languor. . . . For some reason, possibly the fault of the libretto, more

Carl Rosa, founder of the Royal Carl Rosa Opera Company; the company appeared in the New Grand Opera House and Cirque in its first season in 1896, and for many years continued to make annual visits.
GRAND OPERA HOUSE

probably because I could only catch about a third of the words, I failed to discover wherein lay the secret of the trouble, and why Faust and Margaret did not get married. . . . I saw [her] released from the woes of her life, her body stretched on the miserable straw pallet. And with that the walls of her prison rolled back, and I had a vision of her soul being borne through the skies by angels. It is true those white-clad, flaxen-haired creatures, with glistening wings and golden crowns, bore a somewhat unfortunate resemblance to several of the livelier young females I had seen mingling with the soldiers and students at an earlier stage in the drama, nevertheless I beheld them, in this pause in their upward flight, with respect, if not exactly veneration. . . . I resolved I would go to the opera every night that week, but that I would go alone. Between the acts I had eagerly studied my programme, and the unfamiliar, romantic names – *Tannhäuser, Aida, Lohengrin, Rigoletto* – were like sirens singing to me through the darkness, with an irresistible and passionate sweetness.

I went to three more operas that week – listening to them from the gallery, which, if not so pleasant, was less expensive. Then the company departed, and life resumed its normal aspect.

The Royal Carl Rosa Opera Company made a real contribution to the cultural life of Belfast at that time, and judging by Forrest Reid's description of *Faust* they were able to mount elaborate stagings of operas, in quick changes between matinée and evening performances that are not attempted today.

A real challenge for modern stagecraft was enacted in April 1897, when *Lost in New York* was presented. This 'New and Original American Comic Drama', with a great London cast and 'Gorgeous Scenery and Effects', guaranteed its audience that this was a work 'full of Heart Interest, entirely free from clap trap' and promised 'Bright Comedy, New Specialities! The stage converted into a Vast River! Containing over 60,000 Gallons of Real Water! on which will ply Rowboats, Yachts and a Practical Steamboat running at Full Speed.'

Many Victorian theatres were equipped to cope with the extravagant demands of such a spectacle, and the system of water tanks and a stage that could be lowered to accommodate an aquatic scene was linked to the provisions for adapting the stage for the circus. It was not long before the citizens of Belfast were able to see how the New Grand Opera House and Cirque coped with the latter event. On 13 June 1898 the theatre celebrated the grand opening night of the 'Summer Circus Season', under the distinguished patronage of the lord mayor and lady mayoress. Members of the public were reminded that the building could be transformed into a luxurious circus in the 'wonderful short space of 24 hours'. The circus had clowns, acrobats, trapeze artists, monkeys, dogs and a variety of horses, including two Arab horses that had appeared before Queen Victoria by royal command. 'A show to please all! Talent, Excitement, Novelties and Interest! Entirely devoid of Anything approaching Vulgarity!' As J.F. Warden had died earlier in the year, the theatre was now under the management of his son Fred, and a subtle

The New Grand Opera House and Cirque was specifically designed to accommodate the circus. In 1898 a very successful circus was staged and circuses reappeared intermittently until the 1930s.
GRAND OPERA HOUSE

The Grand Circus, the full troupe,
c. 1910
PUBLIC RECORD OFFICE OF
NORTHERN IRELAND

change was about to take place in the theatre, and in its audience.

The enthusiasm for the Grand Opera House itself had been genuine, and was reflected in the many full houses that had been attracted to the theatre. In addition the management had made strenuous efforts to please and accommodate its audience and to keep its standards high, as the *Belfast News-Letter* reported on 3 August 1897:

> The popularity of the Grand Opera House was again attested by the rush to it of large numbers last night on the occasion of its reopening after the summer season. The interior has been 'touched up' by the decorator during the interval, and generally improved. The new entrance that has been made to the dress circle lounge, conducting visitors right into the centre of this sumptuous part of the house, is a change that has been much appreciated.

But in 1898 one or two problems began to emerge under Fred W. Warden's management. The *Belfast News-Letter* launched a diatribe about late arrivals at Carl Rosa's *Tannhäuser* on 5 September. One member of the accused party wrote indignantly that the time of the opening curtain had been wrongly advertised, and so far as they were concerned the company had decided to begin fifteen minutes early. This party had travelled seventy-five miles to be present at the opera, an interesting demonstration not only of the popularity of the theatre and opera but also of the ease of travel.

A further irritation was caused by the introduction of a 7.45 p.m. start for all productions, without regard to the essential matter of late transport. Letters to newspaper editors were written, pointing out the reasonable argument that 'it is during the last quarter of an hour that people wish to enjoy the performance without either the torturing suspense of watching train or tram time, or enduring the discomfort entailed by people (even as it was) necessarily leaving for train or tram'. 'I do not think,' the writer declared, 'that the interests or comfort of those at a distance from the rendezvous of Warden, Limited, have been considered or regarded for one single instant.'

Relations with the press were not ideal, and at this stage of his management, Fred seemed to lack his father's sure touch in public relations. Newspapers that judged productions honestly and critically were not well received. The *Northern Whig* lost its theatre advertisements because of adverse criticism, and subsequently refused to cover theatre matters in its columns at all. A nasty libel case involving Mr Frankfort Moore of the *Belfast News-Letter* soured relations with that newspaper, and the resulting weakness in drama criticism did not help the state of theatrical culture in the city.

In addition to alienating some patrons and the press, the management of the theatre was failing to live up to the cultural aspirations of a section of its audience. Fred Warden became the target of a campaign centred on the fact that Warden Ltd had control of both Belfast's theatres and therefore could dictate the taste of the city. The fashionable periodical the *Magpie* was to the fore in the attack. In December 1898, it wrote, 'Messrs Warden Ltd have a sinecure in Belfast. For here is a town of 300,000 people more or less, and they consider a third-rate music hall show, with fourth-rate vulgarities, good enough for us.' In February 1899, the *Magpie* recommended that the Ulster Hall should be converted into a theatre to provide a viable alternative for audiences. In the same article the periodical analysed the types of entertainment in the Grand Opera House and the Theatre Royal:

In the late 1890s and early 1900s, the journal the *Magpie* and later the *Nomad* gave a political and critical perspective on Belfast life. The writers consistently urged that higher quality drama should be presented in Belfast theatres.

MAGPIE, 1900

To Theatre-Goers.

A ROTTEN SYSTEM OF MONOPOLY IS VITIATING DRAMATIC TASTE IN BELFAST.

(STAR Special).

Whatever may be its claim in other respects to the title of Northern Athens, Belfast has little of that artistic sympathy, of that reverence for the Beautiful which finds its highest expression in the Athens of Pericles. Ulster's capital, like the historical city of ancient Greece, may be the home of trade and the pioneer of commercial enterprise in Ireland, but even the most fanatical admirer of the many good qualities which equip our townsmen for the successful conduct of mercantile concerns, cannot conceal from himself the knowledge—try he ever so hard—that the artistic temperament is not a marked characteristic of the inhabitants of the North-East of Ulster.

BELFAST CENTRAL LIBRARY

Classical Drama	6 weeks
Serious Modern Drama	7 weeks
Grand Opera	2 weeks
Comic Opera	7 weeks
Musical Comedy	20 weeks
First-class Melodramas	13 weeks
Second-class Melodramas	18 weeks
Farcical Comedy	11 weeks
Pantomime	5 weeks
Circus	4 weeks
Negro Minstrels	1 week

Worse still, the *Northern Star* headlined one of its 'Star Special' articles thus: 'To Theatre-Goers. A Rotten System of Monopoly Is Vitiating Dramatic Taste in Belfast'. In an assault which obliquely introduced the national question, the article stated:

It is a matter of regret, to those who had hopes that Belfast would be placed on the same level as cities like Liverpool, Glasgow and Dublin in theatrical affairs that A System of Monopoly has been established of late which destroys any chance of this city being rescued from its theatrical slough of despond . . . In matters connected with the theatre local play-goers are nothing better than so many slaves who are compelled to accept the crumbs that the management of the Theatre Royal and Grand Opera House throw at them. Week after week wretched melodramas, interpreted by fourth-rate companies, visit our theatres. . . . 'The Secrets of the Harem' and 'The Crimes of Paris' are seen in Belfast theatres, but Henry Irving, Forbes-Robertson, and Beerbohm Tree never come nearer than Dublin. . . . It is the intention of THE NORTH-ERN STAR to focus the attention of its readers upon this question, and to demand, in the name of the Nationalists of Belfast – who constitute the over-whelming majority of the patrons of the theatres – that this city shall be placed on a plane with Dublin as regards companies and plays, and that those who cater for the amusement of the public must consult the wishes of the public if they are to continue to receive that popular support upon which they live and have their being.

Matters were not helped by the annual benefit for Fred Warden held in April 1899. This was traditionally an opportunity for thanks and encouragement, and for the announcement of the coming season's engagements. The *Belfast News-Letter* reported the event fully and straightforwardly. A few friends considered that it was a fitting time to make a presentation of a silver tea and coffee set on a silver salver. The gift was intended to encourage him to foster the theatrical art in Belfast, and to convey the assurance that companies capable of attracting the public of this city would be loyally supported.

The *Magpie* was not so bland. An 'Impertinent Personal Letter', one of a series written to eminent citizens, was addressed to Fred Warden. It began thus:

Sir,

I might even say respected sir, because by virtue of being your father's son you could not be otherwise. . . . I cannot say I have been dazzled by the list of engagements entered into for the coming season. I looked in vain for the sign of any break in the traditional and rather monot-onous rut into which theatrical management locally has drifted . . . 'Alone in London' and 'The Silver King' might well give way to Mr Beerbohm Tree, Mrs Patrick Campbell, Mr Alexander, or even Miss Wallis. . . . I congratu-late you upon the mark of warm esteem bestowed upon you at the termina-tion of your speech. It was very pleasant, I am sure, coming 'from a few friends who come in daily contact with you in your business of theatrical management'. How very happily that was put. I could not have improved upon it myself.

You possess a fine theatrical property in Belfast. You have a monopoly; let not your heart be puffed up with too much pride; and remember that the public are indulgent – up to a point, after which – I need say no more.

Proprietor Fred Warden's benefit in 1899; the presentation was intended to encourage him to 'foster the theatrical art' in Belfast.
IRELAND'S SATURDAY NIGHT

A production scene from *The Only Way,* a celebrated adaptation of *A Tale of Two Cities* which was brought to the Grand Opera House on several occasions, the first in 1899.
PUBLIC RECORD OFFICE OF NORTHERN IRELAND

Martin Harvey as Sydney Carton in *The Only Way*
PUBLIC RECORD OFFICE OF NORTHERN IRELAND

In fact the unfavourable comparison of Fred Warden with his father was unfair. J.F. Warden had presented a very similar programme to that of his son, although the critics were right in maintaining that the vast proportion of plays were trivial in the extreme. But Fred Warden continued to bring Carl Rosa, D'Oyly Carte, and Benson, and in October 1899 he engaged Martin Harvey, with Miss de Silva, in a version of *A Tale of Two Cities*. On this occasion the *Magpie* triumphantly asserted, 'The crowded state of the Opera House every night this week amply supports the contention, which I am never tired of driving home, namely that if we were provided with a good class of theatrical fare, we should accord it our thorough support and patronage.' But serious drama without an accompanying big name was poorly supported. The attendances at *The Great Ruby* were 'of the most meagre description', according to the *Magpie*, a state of affairs which the writer put down to the irregularity of good shows:

The Messrs Warden ruin their reputation by bringing shows which you wouldn't ask even boiled cats to witness; then when something decent comes along it is hung with a bad name . . . unless of course, it has a special reputation of itself – like 'The Geisha' or 'The Greek Slave'. It is of little wonder that many theatre companies regard Belfast as a town of 'frost' and no wonder that the best companies refuse to come here at all.

The financial outlook was worsening, too. It was reported by the *Magpie* that there was great dissatisfaction among holders of the annual debenture tickets at the Theatre Royal and the Grand Opera House because of the quality of the shows. A good cast had been gathered for the stock, or repertory, season at the Theatre Royal, but the plays they were to act in were derided. The *Magpie* added that the average attendance was poor and on no occasion was the Theatre Royal more than one third full. A report in *Ireland's Saturday Night* contradicts this, and gives more credit to Fred Warden for his enterprise in experimenting with a stock season.

Indisputably, the revival of the stock season at the Theatre Royal has been a success, and has quite justified Mr Fred Warden in embarking on what was regarded by many as a somewhat risky enterprise. Mr Warden tells me that he has been inundated with letters from brother managers from all over the

United Kingdom, who are anxious to know how the experiment has resulted, and he has been able to give a favourable reply. A good criterion is the receipts, and this season a profit has been made, which has never been done before in the summer season.

The running of a stock season means very hard work for all concerned – managers and company. While a piece is running to which the players were probably strangers the previous week, it is necessary for the coming week's production to be in rehearsal. The procedure in getting up a play, Mr Warden kindly explained to me, is as follows: On Monday the cast is put up, and the parts are given out. On Tuesday parts are compared and the first rough rehearsal takes place on Wednesday. The second rehearsal on Thursday is a bit 'cleaner', Friday's and Saturday's are almost if not altogether perfect, and on Monday morning, there is a full rehearsal with scenery, properties, dresses, and music – just the same performance as is to be given before the audience that night.

Warden's general reliance on the popular end of the market is understandable. Despite the vociferous lobby for higher quality, audience figures certainly did not always justify the expense of bringing the best. Even the ever-popular Royal Carl Rosa Opera Company failed to gain maximum houses in September 1899. The *Magpie*'s correspondent reported thus:

> I regret to hear, on good authority, that the audiences were not what they might have been. There was one good house – on Friday night – but then Friday night is not a guide. There are a certain class who go to the theatre on that particular night merely because it is the correct thing to do, and it would not matter what company or what opera was appearing, they would be there just the same. . . . But if we gauge the musical culture of Belfast by the average attendance of the week, I fear we will not be able to congratulate ourselves.

Miss de Silva in *The Only Way, c.* 1899
PUBLIC RECORD OFFICE OF
NORTHERN IRELAND

The £5 shares of the company had by now fallen to £2 17s. 6d., and in the last year of J.F. Warden's guarantee the trustees had to be called in to make good a substantial deficit, in contrast to the theatre's first year, when profits had exceeded the guarantee. The Warden Theatres were not alone in their financial difficulties –- the Ulster Hall had also failed to pay its way in 1899 and the Alhambra was up for sale – but as Fred Warden looked towards a new century, he must have wondered whether the prudent course would be a change of direction.

3
TEMPLE OF THESPIS,
OR TWICE-NIGHTLY VARIETY?

FRED WARDEN BEGAN THE NEW CENTURY with a slight, but important change to the name of his principal theatre. Now the New Grand Opera House and Cirque was officially described as the Grand Opera House, and there were sure signs that the theatre would test the market for better drama and more celebrated actors. The year started well, with the usual post-pantomime appearance of Frank Benson, complete with a *Hamlet*, which the actor managed to revive perennially. This time the exacting critic of the *Magpie* decided that 'the entire presentation of the play has been carefully thought out from a scholar's standpoint and nothing better has ever been seen in the provinces'. Benson gave his Belfast admirers something of a challenge when he presented *The Tempest*, acting the part of Caliban. 'The audience was large on Tuesday but were scarcely certain what to make of it.'

A month later the same critic let himself down when he went to see *Lady Windermere's Fan*.

> *Lady Windermere's Fan* has strayed from St James' Theatre, London, and I wish it would stray back again. . . . it is described in the programme as a successful play, but the author's name is not given. . . . it is in the hands of a painfully unsuitable cast. . . . I was unable to sit through the more than two acts.

Oscar Wilde's play is one of the very few works of that period that is still viewed by theatre audiences today.

The Grand Opera House productions during the spring of 1900 included the usual light ingredients. *Little Miss Nobody* was dismissed as 'inanity, inanity, all is inanity – in musical comedy. Take a small plot – very small and boil it down until it disappears. This will do for stock. Add any quality of supposed to be comic songs and topical duets. Dress gorgeously and serve with a hash of mixed music and some sentimental ballads thrown in.' Next came *Frivolity* – 'comedians in the Pantomimical, Farcical, Musical Absurdity', and *The Tyranny of Tears*, of which one critic wrote, 'Mr Hadden Chambers' play is on the thinnest of subjects, and it was played on Monday to a thinner house.' Another light piece was *High Jinks*; the *Magpie*'s critic gives a sardonic description of this typical piece of light entertainment.

> I sat down beside a man who shivered during the entire performance of 'High Jinks'. I am not yet certain whether he was in pain or enjoying himself, because you see, I sort of enjoyed myself at first, and was afterwards in mental pain, when the jinks got monotonous, though I did not quite get to

Opposite:
Mrs Patrick Campbell, George Bernard Shaw's favourite actress, one of the many celebrities whom Fred Warden brought to Belfast after 1901
THEATRE MUSEUM, V. & A.

THE D'OYLY CARTE OPERA COMPANY

GRAND OPERA HOUSE

the length of shivering. The first scene is at a popular seaside resort. Bevy after bevy of young and lovely girls waltz on and sing. They are dressed in a fashion which I would very much question if the local authorities would sanction. Visions of white and pink with robes of blue and light greens, red and mauve, and long and shapely legs, peeping out here and there are nice – but they do get monotonous after a time. . . . 'High Jinks' stays for a fortnight and is worth looking at if you have nothing better to do.

The Moody Manners Opera Company came with *Lohengrin*, *Faust*, and *Lily of Killarney*, and D'Oyly Carte came immediately before an Easter pantomime of *Cinderella*, and the reliable box office success *San Toy*. It is worth looking at the competition in the shape of the Ulster Hall, where in April Clara Butt sang, as one critic wrote, to a 'fairly good but most unappreciative audience. Miss Butt was in fine form and I have never heard her magnificent contralto to better advantage.' In the same month the Ulster Hall housed 'the latest and up-to-date Boer War Myriorama – a revelation of startling and pleasing delights – Colenso, gallant effort to save the guns, [and] Terrors of Johannesburg'.

Sir Henry Irving's first visit to the Grand Opera House in 1901 was hugely successful. Belfast was said to have suffered an attack of 'Irving on the Brain'.
THEATRE MUSEUM, V. & A.

But at Fred Warden's benefit in May 1900 and again at his benefit in 1901, more exciting fare for the Grand Opera House was forecast, in a programme that included the best theatrical companies and popular entertainment. This was to be the quality fare for which the critics had clamoured for so long. In the period between 1900 and 1904, the Grand Opera House presented Johnston Forbes-Robertson, Lillie Langtry, Herbert Beerbohm Tree, Mrs Patrick Campbell, George Alexander, Henry Irving and Ellen Terry. It was to be a golden period for lovers of fine drama.

At the same time Warden Ltd promised to continue to bring the regular opera companies and the most popular musical comedies. The proportion of plays that delighted in the descriptions 'screamingly funny farcical comedy' or 'new and modern extravaganza' was much lower than in the previous years. Two genuinely popular shows were well supported. Despite the change in the title of the theatre, the Royal Italian Circus came with a hundred animals, clowns, trapeze artists and tightrope walkers. The pantomime *The Sleeping Beauty* was such an outstanding success that it led to an unprecedented dispute involving the recently formed trades council, of which more below.

The quality of this pantomime won the admiration of the prestigious London-based periodical the *Stage,* which wrote that 'the flourishing city on the Lagan is being treated to a pantomime which, in a word, is in advance of what has been for many years submitted for its approval'. The article praised the enterprise of Fred Warden in his efforts to 'convince the good people of a city noted for its linen and shipbuilding that it is their duty to support the local stage', and commended the pantomime's quality, 'regardless of expense', with 'costumes which brought the house down' and 'a few good old gags, municipal, social or topical', although the *Stage* was surprised at the complete absence of references to the Boer War, which was providing fodder for jokes at pantomimes throughout England.

The pantomime was so popular that those wishing to avail of the 'early door' experienced considerable difficulty. A letter to the editor of the *Belfast News-Letter* from 'Reform' deplored the chaotic state outside the door. His grievance was that he had arrived with his family in good time for the pit door, but the crowd had been so large and the crush so unbearable that there was great disappointment for many who had stood with children. In the end 'Reform' had decided to return home with his children 'while their bones were whole, rather than run the risk of personal injury and getting the children trampled upon'. The writer's main complaint was against the police, who, he felt, were failing in their duty.

The management of the Grand Opera House endeavoured to cope with the huge numbers attending the pantomime, and provided the crowded early houses with electric animated photographs while they waited for the pantomime to begin. The trades council dispute arose because the orchestra was asked to play during the pre-performance entertainments, but was not offered any extra payment. The orchestra refused to comply, and during the subsequent court action it emerged that the Dublin orchestra, playing under identical circumstances when the pantomime was transferred there, received a supplement to their wages. The row rumbled on for several months, during which time the theatre had to operate with a much-reduced musical accompaniment.

Other complaints surfaced during this period. The first was the recurring problem of the conduct of the occupants of the gods. Traditionally, the gods was a good-natured, if inevitably rowdy area of the theatre, and it must be remembered that, as Matcham had designed it, twice as many people occupied the gallery as do today. An example of the wit of the gallery earned a guinea for James Moore of Southview Street in Belfast, in the columns of the *Ireland's Saturday Night* of 7 April 1900, with this 'storyette':

> The other evening 'High Jinks' was being performed in the Grand Opera House, Belfast. The view of the stage and actors was obstructed by a man standing up, seemingly deaf to all the hissing and booing behind him. At last came the voice, 'Let the poor fellow alone! Shure he's a poor tailor, and is only resting himself.'

Occasionally it went too far. 'A Sufferer' writing to the *Northern Whig* about behaviour when Frank Benson was visiting lamented 'the scandalous conduct of the denizens of the gallery during the entire intervals between the acts, keeping up continually great disorder, and for a time turning the gallery into a pandemonium deafening and ear-splitting, with every description of noise'. At least it appears that they were quiet during the play, which could not be said for a 'respectable looking man' named Joseph Whitelaw, who was charged in the Belfast Custody Court with riotous behaviour. The man was not intoxicated, but he kept up a racket to the annoyance of the audience. Whitelaw's defence was that he disapproved of the play, which was *The Little Minister* by J.M. Barrie, and had a perfect right to do so. The magistrates did not agree, and he was fined 21s.

In a letter to the *Belfast News-Letter*, 'Chaperone' urged Warden to call in the police after witnessing the worst behaviour from the gallery when she accompanied a group of young ladies to the pantomime in 1902. Although she appreciated that 'from time immemorial license has been permitted to the "gods" and even captious critics have withheld censure when speaking of their histrionic playfulness', she felt that on this occasion the bounds of decency were passed: 'party expressions of the grossest description which if uttered on the public street would be punished with "40s. or a month" were freely indulged in'.

Another source of contention was the problem of the large hats worn by the ladies of the late-Victorian era, which often obscured the view of those behind. A campaign to persuade ladies to remove their hats was started in London and transferred to Belfast, with a notice on the curtain reminding them of the inconvenience caused. This latter was viewed with some annoyance by a lady writer in the *Belfast News-Letter* in February 1901, who wrote indignantly as follows:

Was it necessary on Monday Night at the Opera House to be again reminded of a little part in etiquette which I spoke of last week? We, as ladies, should know what to do without being reminded in such a forcible manner. I do hope after this week we shall not want such a reminder as a curtain staring at us with these words: 'Madam, will you kindly take off your hat, as I am sitting behind you and cannot see the Stage.'

In the next decade every programme would include a paragraph about the wearing of hats.

The question of dress was a factor in the prices of admission. Warden decided that from September 1900 the front rows of the circle should be reserved for people in evening dress at a charge of four shillings, while the charge for the rows behind, which could also be reserved and in which ladies might wear bonnets, would be reduced to three shillings. It was felt that this arrangement would tend to popularise the circle, which was less favoured than the stalls. A year later, at his benefit, Fred Warden announced that the Theatre Royal would reduce its prices – leaving the Grand Opera House as the implied destination for quality. 'My brother directors are with me in the opinion that the masses should be catered for as well as the classes, and with this in view we have decided to reduce the prices in the Theatre Royal. . . . in making this experiment we hope it will mark the commencement of a new era in our theatrical

Ellen Terry as Juliet; in 1901 Belfast audiences flocked to see her memorable partnership with Sir Henry Irving in *The Merchant of Venice*.
THEATRE MUSEUM, V. & A.

enterprise.' He announced that all the leading stars of the theatrical world would visit, and added, with portent, 'From the forthcoming list, ladies and gentlemen, I am sure you will agree with me that Belfast never has been so well provided for before, and it will rest with the theatrical-going public to say whether or not these attractions will return to us in the year 1902.' The Belfast public was being placed on its mettle, and it was widely expected that its reception of this promised galaxy of stars – Irving, Terry, Tree, Forbes-Robertson, Langtry, Campbell and Alexander – would be significant for the theatre of the future.

Grand Opera House

GREAT VICTORIA STREET, BELFAST.

Proprietors, ... "WARDEN, LIMITED."
Managing Director, ... FRED W. WARDEN.
Acting Manager, ... W. J. ANDREWS.

Week Commencing MONDAY, FEBRUARY 4th, 1901.

HENRY IRVING,
MISS
ELLEN TERRY
AND THE LONDON LYCEUM COMPANY.

THIS EVENING—Shakespeare's Comedy, in Five Acts,

Matinee The
Merchant of Venice

GRAND OPERA HOUSE

In the meantime, a new director had been appointed for Warden Ltd: Mr Frederick Mouillot was a gentleman who had evidently plenty of good connections, and was able to establish a professional working relationship with the Theatre Royal, Dublin. The local critic 'Quiz' met Mouillot after the first visit of Sir Henry Irving, and asked if he thought that the visit of Sir Henry would have beneficial effects. Mouillot's reply was positive:

> Yes, distinctly. It will show the other great stars that they can safely bring their large companies with their heavy scenery and accessories as the receipts will justify the expenditure. The theatres in Belfast have been working under a cloud, because it was so difficult to get any of the great actors to go out of the beaten track, because they could not understand that Belfast had grown so rapidly as it has during the last ten years.
>
> The directors are now making arrangements . . . and in the next twelve or eighteen months, will have the whole of the London stars. Then, once it becomes a regular institution, they are sure to visit Belfast on each of their tours. . . . I think I may speak for the directors when I say that all we want is the help of the Belfast people, that when the great actors and actresses do come they will be supported in the same way as Sir Henry Irving has been. . . . Actors and actresses are like everyone else – they have to live. Unless the public support them they must go where they can get their bread and butter – with occasionally a little bit of jam spread on it.

The great experiment with Belfast public taste got off to a splendid start with the visit of Sir Henry Irving and Ellen Terry in February 1901. Despite an increase in prices the houses were excellent, and the reception was rapturous. The stature and influence of Irving was enormous. In 1895 he had become the first actor to be knighted, an honour which was seen, in a society much concerned with respectability, to have placed a final and unquestionable seal of Establishment approval on the acting profession. Irving was celebrated for his Shakespearean roles and as a historical purist had played a pioneering role in restoring a great number of plays to their original text, after many years of performance in excised and altered versions. As an actor his style

The famous actor Johnston Forbes-Robertson was brought to the Grand Opera House by Fred Warden in 1901 in response to calls for a higher quality programme. When he came, however, the houses were poor.
THEATRE MUSEUM, V. & A.

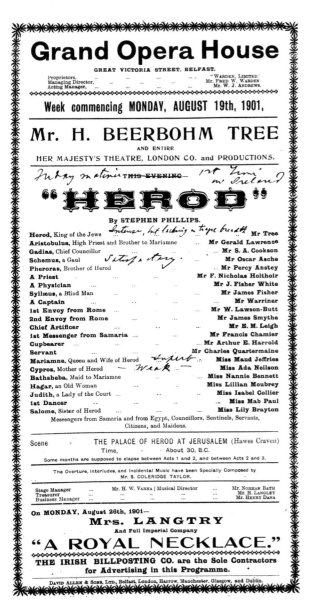

Grand Opera House

GREAT VICTORIA STREET, BELFAST.

Proprietors, ... "WARDEN, LIMITED."
Managing Director, ... Mr. FRED W. WARDEN.
Acting Manager, ... Mr. W. J. ANDREWS.

Week commencing MONDAY, AUGUST 19th, 1901,

Mr. H. BEERBOHM TREE

AND ENTIRE
HER MAJESTY'S THEATRE, LONDON CO. and PRODUCTIONS.

Friday matinée THIS EVENING — *1st Time in Ireland*

"HEROD"

By STEPHEN PHILLIPS.

Herod, King of the Jews *Intense, but lacking in type breadth*	Mr Tree
Aristobulus, High Priest and Brother to Mariamne	... Mr Gerald Lawrence
Gadias, Chief Councillor	... Mr S. A. Cookson
Schemus, a Gaul *Satisfactory.*	Mr Oscar Asche
Pheroras, Brother of Herod	Mr Percy Anstey
A Priest	Mr F. Nicholas Holthoir
A Physician	Mr J. Fisher White
Syllæus, a Blind Man ...	Mr James Fisher
A Captain ...	Mr Warriner
1st Envoy from Rome	Mr W. Lawson-Butt
2nd Envoy from Rome ...	Mr James Smythe
Chief Artificer	Mr E. M. Leigh
1st Messenger from Samaria ...	Mr Francis Chamier
Cupbearer	Mr Arthur E. Harrold
Servant	Mr Charles Quartermaine
Mariamne, Queen and Wife of Herod *Superb* ..	Miss Maud Jeffries
Cypros, Mother of Herod *Weak*	Miss Ada Neilson
Bathsheba, Maid to Mariamne	Miss Nannie Bennett
Hagar, an Old Woman	Miss Lillian Moubrey
Judith, a Lady of the Court ...	Miss Isabel Collier
1st Dancer	... Miss Mab Paul
Salome, Sister of Herod	Miss Lily Brayton

Messengers from Samaria and from Egypt, Councillors, Sentinels, Servants,
Citizens, and Maidens.

Scene - THE PALACE OF HEROD AT JERUSALEM (Hawes Craven)
Time, - About 30, B.C.
Some months are supposed to elapse between Acts 1 and 2, and between Acts 2 and 3.

The Overture, Interludes, and Incidental Music have been Specially Composed by
Mr. S. COLERIDGE TAYLOR.

Stage Manager	... Mr. H. W. VARNA	Musical Director	... Mr. NORMAN BATH
Treasurer			Mr. H. LANGLEY
Business Manager	...		Mr. HENRY DANA

On MONDAY, August 26th, 1901,—

Mrs. LANGTRY

And Full Imperial Company

"A ROYAL NECKLACE."

THE IRISH BILLPOSTING CO. are the Sole Contractors
for Advertising in this Programme.

DAVID ALLEN & SONS, LTD., Belfast, London, Harrow, Manchester, Glasgow, and Dublin.

Annotated programme in a collection of
theatre memorabilia made by a Victorian
play-goer, remarking on the strengths and
weaknesses of respective performances
BELFAST CENTRAL LIBRARY

was said to have been highly mannered and hugely magnetic. His legendary partnership with Ellen Terry had begun when she joined his Lyceum Company in 1878, and was to continue only until 1902, so the Belfast audiences of 1901 were very fortunate to have caught a performance by this famous pair. Ellen Terry was often self-deprecating: 'I am not a great actress, I am not indeed. I am only a very useful one to Henry.' But Sybil Thorndike said of her, 'The perfect symbol in her work is what the true theatre is – an instrument which transformed body, voice, clothes, words, all materials into spirit – spiritual essence.' It was said that she spoke Shakespeare as if she had just been talking to him in the next room.

In July, Mrs Patrick Campbell came with *Mariana*. It has to be said that this celebrated and charismatic actress was not the most enthusiastic theatrical tourer. On one occasion she wrote to Lilian Braithwaite when she was playing a character based on the famous Mrs Pat, 'Oh, Lilian, I hear you are a perfect *tour de force* playing me! And here I am forced to tour.'

In August, Belfast prepared to receive Beerbohm Tree. It was not perhaps the best time of the year for a visiting star. Belfast theatres were used to closing for the summer, the citizens of the city leaving for the flourishing seaside resorts and coming back with their pockets empty, and there was not the usual service of late tramcars. Whatever the reason, the Grand Opera House was strangely empty for this momentous visit. The London *Sunday Times* glowered, 'It will be unquestionably to the discredit of the Belfast public if more liberal patronage be not extended to Mr Tree and his company during the remainder of their short stay in their city.'

The *Northern Whig*, now covering the theatre again, was in despair. Writing on 21 August, its critic lamented at some length:

Lovers of the drama with a sincere regard for the progress of the art in Belfast could not help having a feeling of pain at the miserably inadequate attendance at the Grand Opera House last evening. We have at present with us one of the most famous companies of the world, headed by a gentleman whose fame is second to none . . . and yet he had to play to benches little more than half full. . . . Complaints have been made that the drama at its highest level is rarely, if ever, presented here. If there is any justification for this grievance, our local theatre manager is sincerely endeavouring to find a remedy and it is a sad reflection that at the start of this new policy a rebuff has been administered. The law of supply and demand regulates most things and Mr Warden, after having given us a good trial, can hardly be blamed if this city sinks into the position of a third-rate town, where nothing could possibly attract a curious public but so-called musical comedy and the lowest of vulgar melodrama.

A telling factor emerged. It was the popular seats in the house that were being sold, and the expensive ones that remained empty. The apathetic middle classes of Belfast were responsible for this cultural embarrassment. Beerbohm Tree himself took the situation with apparent good humour. On the closing night of the tour, when a full house had reacted with enormous enthusiasm to *Herod*, Tree came out to give his customary speech, which the *Belfast Evening Telegraph* recorded in full.

He expressed his gratification for the splendid reception, as he did not think the piece had ever gone with greater appreciation than it had that night.

Sir Herbert Beerbohm Tree as Svengali; when he visited Belfast in 1901, the Grand Opera House audiences were disappointing. However, said Tree, 'there was more joy over full houses at the end of the week than sorrow over comparatively empty ones at the beginning'.
THEATRE MUSEUM, V. & A.

> It was particularly gratifying because he was told that Belfast audiences were not given to classical drama. (A Voice – 'Nonsense'.) He confessed that in the early part of the week he was disappointed that the houses were not quite full, but that splendid audience recorded their victory (cheers) and there was more joy over full houses at the end of the week than there was sorrow over the comparatively empty ones at the beginning. (Hear, hear.) Then he was told it was a pity he did not come with a musical comedy (laughter) and he replied that surely the 'Twelfth Night', if it was anything, was a musical comedy. (Applause.) He hoped they would become better acquainted and that their friendship would increase in future years. (Applause.) He should be very proud if he could be one of those who contributed, however humbly, to the revival of a love of theatre in this great city (cheers).

Another view of this actor's performance is supplied by an avid theatre-goer whose collection of programmes and press cuttings is held in good order in Belfast Central Library, forming a very useful archive. Some of his programmes contain notes, and in *Herod*, which the spectator saw at a matinée performance, Tree had to be prompted twice, and his interpretation was considered 'intense, but lacking tragic breadth'.

Belfast's lack of appreciation of Beerbohm Tree must have been something more than an irritant to this actor whose ironic attitude to vanity was famous. He was said to have remarked, 'The only man who wasn't spoiled by being lionised was Daniel', and 'When I pass my name in such large letters, I blush, but at the same time instinctively raise my hat.'

Good humour about poor houses was in generous supply at that time. The story goes that Edward Terry, who also came to the Grand Opera House in 1901, played before a very meagre audience in the Opera House in Derry. During the performance, fire engines raced past to a building nearby, and there was some unease in the stalls. Terry stepped forward to the footlights, raised his hand, and said, 'Don't be alarmed, ladies and gentlemen; there's a window for each of you.' Mrs Patrick Campbell's favourite remark, when faced with a thin house, was, 'The Marquess and

In 1901 the floods which engulfed Great Victoria Street, including the Great Northern Railway terminus, disrupted the important visit of George Alexander's company. It was one of the factors which led to financial disaster at the Grand Opera House, and its change of name to the Palace of Varieties.

ULSTER FOLK AND TRANSPORT MUSEUM

IRELAND'S SATURDAY NIGHT

Marchioness of empty are in front again.'

But there could be no excuses of holidays or late transport when Forbes-Robertson played to poor houses in October, and the serious loss incurred for Beerbohm Tree and later Mrs Langtry was repeated, even though the lord and lady mayoress, Sir Robert and Lady McConnell, held a reception in his honour at their home in Strandtown for 150 guests, many of whom had never been in the theatre, it was said. The next lord mayor and lady mayoress, Sir Daniel and Lady Dixon, tried again to lead opinion on the visit of George Alexander in November, when this time 600 guests were invited to an 'at home' at the town hall. Alexander's visit began as a great success. The audience was large and fashionable and the popular repertoire proved a winner. This time an Oscar Wilde play was well presented and received, and the house 'convulsed with laughter as never before' to *The Importance of Being Earnest*. Then really bad luck hit the theatre management. George Alexander fell ill following a routine vaccination and was unable to appear. Then natural disaster struck. A terrible storm flooded all the streets around the Grand Opera House, and submerged the stage itself under water. Performances that were salvaged were transferred to the Theatre Royal. Fred Warden's experiment in testing the taste of the public had been fraught with problems, and the fate of first-class drama in Belfast was sealed for a decade.

It was no surprise when, in 1904, Warden Limited transferred all

The Grand Opera House, called the Palace
of Varieties between 1904 and 1909,
advertising its twice-nightly variety shows
NATIONAL LIBRARY OF IRELAND

serious drama to the smaller Theatre Royal, and the Grand Opera House, catering for the more lucrative trade, was renamed the Palace of Varieties and began to provide twice-nightly variety programmes. The *Nomad*, the successor to the *Magpie*, reported that Warden had chosen as his model the Hippodrome and Palace in London, adding that the decision to put on two performances each night was sensible because 'the proximity of the Palace to the Ulster Railway terminus should ensure a good audience of country visitors for the first performance, while for us "townies", it will, no doubt, become the fashion to drop into the Palace for the 9.00 show'. The weekly matinée was at 2.30 p.m. so that it would not clash with the Royal, Empire or Hippodrome, and the tickets were very cheap, 3d. to 1s. 6d. A typical show in 1904 included minstrels, 'the world's stump orator', an eccentric comedian, dancers, a burlesque tragedian, a banjo eccentric, and the jubileeo-graph, 'introducing all the latest pictures in animated photography'.

PALACE THEATRE OF VARIETIES

2—PERFORMANCES NIGHTLY—2
At 7 and 9 p.m.
☞ MATINEE WEDNESDAY AT 2-30. ☜
Admission, 3d to 1s 6d.

NOMAD

It was the zenith of the music-hall, and it seemed that there was an unquenchable supply of acts for an insatiable audience. Thus in 1904 it appeared to the *Nomad* that the Opera House had 'seen the last of its days as a theatre of legitimate drama, while the Theatre Royal is preparing to enter upon a new lease of life as Belfast's one and only Thespian Temple'.

The novelty of some acts led to trouble. On one occasion 'The Cowboy

Sarah Bernhardt, who made several 'flying' visits to the Grand Opera House in the early twentieth century
THEATRE MUSEUM, V. & A.

Grand Opera House.

MONDAY Next, FEBRUARY 1st, Six Nights,
Matinee Friday, February 5th, at 2.

The Gorgeous Musical Play

" *Butterflies*, "

From the Apollo Theatre, London.

Full Chorus and Augmented Orchestra.

Prices, **6d.** to **4/-**   Box Office daily, **10 to 3.**

NOMAD

Hypnotist' was on the bill, and the performer in question advertised his act by marching round the city every lunchtime with a band. His alleged hypnotic powers were exposed as fraudulent, and his angry dupes wrecked the gallery of the theatre in revenge.

Even while the twice-nightly variety programme was the staple diet, however, Warden continued to use the Palace as a venue, especially for the 'flying visit' performances that became a feature of the theatre at this time, when a celebrated personality would fit in a matinée between appearances in Dublin and Scotland. Martin Harvey came in 1905, in *A Cigarette Maker's Romance*, and he came again in 1906 in *The Only Way*.

In spite of roaring wind and rain, there was such a house at the Palace as would delight the heart of the most pessimistic manager. Scarcely an empty seat in the Dress Circle, the parterre a sea of heads, and from the gallery, full handed thunders of applause that showed the gods had more than done their duty.

Mrs Patrick Campbell made a brief visit in 1907, and then came Sarah Bernhardt in *The Lady of the Camellias*: 'She is as ever, Sarah, the divine, the incomparable; graceful in motion, unaffected in style, superb in repose. Her voice has its old and wonderful charm, and even in its lowest tones it thrills and enchants the hearer by its marvellous sweetness.' Occasionally the Royal Carl Rosa Opera Company performed at the Palace and for *Il Trovatore* it was advertised that the South African and Irish rugby fifteens would be present.

But by 1909 it was all change again. On 30 January, advertisements appeared returning the Grand Opera House to its rightful title, and starting the season with *Butterflies*, 'a Gorgeous Musical Play', followed, and no doubt the juxtaposition was intended, by *Moths*, 'a Great Realistic Human Play'. Up went the prices again, to the old rates of 6d. to 4s., while those at the Theatre Royal plummeted to 4d. to 1s. 6d. as it presented *How Girls Are Brought to Ruin*, 'New Sensational Drama, smoking permitted'. Improvements had been made to the theatre: 'the spacious and commodious house had been subjected to artistic decoration and everything had been done to cater for the comfort of all patrons, while the stage had been overhauled and a delightful drop-act had been specially painted by the clever and versatile resident scenic artist, Mr Gustave Jansen'. The year continued very much as years had in the old days. Carl Rosa came and so did D'Oyly Carte, bringing *Princess Ida* to 'an audience of an appreciative type not too often recognised in Belfast, who proved that they were critical and discriminating'. Although the quality of visitors never reached the dizzy heights of 1901, 'important engagements' included Martin Harvey. The Celebrated Compton Comedy Company brought a nice blend of

Sheridan, Goldsmith and contemporary comedy, and Benson made another of his pilgrimages to the city. When the George Edwardes Company brought *The Merry Widow*, in September 1909, circle prices went up to 5s. and 4s., but it is worth noting that when Caruso sang in the same month at the Ulster Hall, concert-goers were asked to spend between 7s. 6d. and 21s. to hear the legend.

This period also saw something completely different in the theatres of Belfast. For the first time, audiences were invited to see drama that sprang from an Irish, and from an Ulster, tradition. The history of the Abbey Theatre is well documented elsewhere. Its players made their first of many visits to Belfast in 1908, to the Theatre Royal, and in 1910, they appeared on the Grand Opera House stage for the first time, with a variety of plays including *Riders to the Sea*, *The Rising of the Moon*, and *The Well of the Saints*. The visit went extremely well, but the *Northern Whig* was just a little caustic in its comments.

> It took the Abbey players a long time to nerve themselves for a raid North of the Boyne. They tackled London, Manchester and Cambridge light-heartedly enough but they seemed to imagine that Ulster was still as fiercely hostile to a southern invasion as when Cuchullain guarded the passes against Queen Maeve. . . . Not until the Ulster Theatre had shown them the way by beating up their quarters in Dublin did they pluck up heart for their adventure, to find they had been jibbing at an open door. The result was a triumph. A well-filled house gave a warm welcome both to plays and to players.

The Ulster Literary Theatre (ULT) mentioned in the *Northern Whig* review presented its first plays on the stage of the Grand Opera House in May 1909, announcing itself 'in repertoire' for the first time. The company, which in 1924 changed its name to the Ulster Theatre, drew inspiration, but not always encouragement, from the Irish Literary Theatre of Yeats. In fact, the new company was forced to change its name from the Ulster Branch of the Irish Literary Theatre following objections from Dublin. The leading figures in the formation of the ULT were Bulmer Hobson and David Parkhill (Lewis Purcell), who in 1902 went down to Dublin to see what Yeats and the Fays were up to and came back resolving to do likewise, namely both to bring the former's new plays to Belfast and to write and produce new plays themselves. Maud Gonne played a significant part in their beginnings, according to Bulmer Hobson.

> Parkhill and I wanted to get in touch with the National Theatre Society, which had been started by Maud Gonne's Daughters of Eireann. The Fays were the producers and Yeats, AE and all the writing crowd were actively helping. . . . We wanted permission to put on some of their plays and help from some of their actors. Everybody was most cordial and helpful except Yeats – haughty and aloof. . . . we wanted to put on in Belfast 'Kathleen ni Houlihan', and O'Cuisin's 'The Racing Lug'. Dudley Digges and Maire Quin promised to come and act in our first production. But Yeats refused permission. When Maire reported this to Maud Gonne, Maud said, 'Don't

The Abbey Theatre made their first visit to the Grand Opera House in 1910; they were well received and continued to enjoy enthusiastic receptions throughout the century.
GRAND OPERA HOUSE

mind Willie. He wrote that play for me and gave it to me. It is mine and you can put it on whenever you want to.' So (in 1902) we put on 'Kathleen ni Houlihan' and 'The Racing Lug' with Dudley Digges and Maire Quin as our leading actors. Annoyed by Yeats we decided to write our own plays – and we did.

This first production was presented in St Mary's Hall, Bank Street, in 1902.

The first performances of the Ulster Literary Theatre took place before sparse audiences, but the theatre followed a new direction in 1904 when it launched the first issue of *Uladh*, described as 'an Ulster Literary Review', which had among its contributors Padraic Colum, James Connolly, Alice Milligan, Roger Casement, AE and Stephen Gwynn, as well as the stalwarts of the company: Joseph and John Campbell, George and Norman Morrow, and Francis Joseph Bigger.

The first editorial announced:

SAM M·KINSTRY.

Sam McKinstry, a character in Lewis Purcell's *The Enthusiast*, which was produced by the Ulster Literary Theatre in 1909. The drawing is by Norman Morrow.
ULADH

We in Belfast and Ulster also wish to set up a school . . . at present we can only say that our talent is more satiric than poetic. That will probably remain the broad difference between the Ulster and Leinster schools. But when our genius arrives, as he must sooner or later, there is no accounting for what extraordinary tendency he may display. . . . There is a strong undercurrent of culture in the North and this we will endeavour to tap, and if possible turn into native channels. If we succeed in this much, if we awaken the people to sympathy and life, surely our existence will be justified.

There was a consistently strong regional bias in all *Uladh*'s activities, strong enough to cause James Connolly to ask it to consider whether its aim should not be to interpret Ulster to the rest of Ireland rather than build barriers between it and the other provinces.

Another article in *Uladh* highlighted the persistent problem of the perception of the theatre in the North.

In Dublin, the project for a national theatre was bound to find many supporters from the first. There drama has always been a force, and new ideas, even in the darkest days of reaction, have been granted a hearing. Here we guard ourselves against new ideas as against a plague. The theatre is not recognised, but merely tolerated, and the idea that the stage may afford a medium for the expression of national sentiment, as vital and sincere as a great poem or a great picture, would be regarded by thousands as little short of blasphemy.

After the launch of *Uladh* the members began to write themselves, in a form derivative of the works coming from Dublin. Bulmer Hobson's *Brian of Banba* and Joseph Campbell's *The Little Cowherd of Slainge* were verse plays, and by all accounts they were very bad, the only redeeming feature being the acting of the female roles. The works of Lewis Purcell were much more successful. *The Enthusiast* and *The Pagan* used the language and style of speech of Ulster, and Forrest Reid, writing years later, described *The Enthusiast* as a 'genuine work of art – slight, imperfect, but vital'. *Uladh* regarded Mr Purcell's dialogue as 'pre-eminently natural to the people whom he has depicted, and there is not a dead line in it', considering that 'it is so essentially an Ulster play that it requires Ulster actors for its proper interpretation'.

In 1906, Rutherford Mayne's *Turn o' the Road* took the Ulster Literary Theatre one step towards Ulster naturalistic drama, and in 1908, the theatre made its first visit to Dublin. The Belfast author David Kennedy, writing in 1951 in *The Arts in Ulster*, argued that the ULT's influence on Irish drama may have been underestimated.

> The success of Mayne, Lynn Doyle, and other members of the Ulster Theatre in the kitchen comedy may have been a more vital influence on the development of the art of the drama in Ireland than has ever been acknowledged by historians of the theatre. When the Ulster Theatre visited Dublin in 1908 with some of these plays, *The Irish Times* wrote: 'We seem to be on the verge of a revolution in dramatic art, and remarkably enough, it has been left to Ulster to lead the way.' The kitchen comedy and the naturalistic acting which made the Abbey Theatre famous are a long way removed from the ideals which the young Yeats first brought to the Irish Literary Theatre.

Suzanne and the Sovereigns by Gerald MacNamara, one of the most successful comedies produced by the Ulster Literary Theatre
NOMAD, 1909

The Ulster Literary Theatre not only addressed the language and life of the Ulster scene, but also attempted to handle some of the themes and conflicts that have troubled it. Purcell's play *The Pagan* broached mixed marriage between Protestants and Catholics, dealing with the sensitivity of the subject by placing it at a distance of one thousand years. Gerald MacNamara (Harry Morrow) switched the time scale and drew on a rich vein of humour by bringing subjects of the past into the present. Some of his most successful plays, like *Suzanne and the Sovereigns*, *Thompson in Tir-na-nOg* and *No Surrender*, in which William III and the Orange Order made surprising appearances, were revived repeatedly. In *Thompson in Tir-na-nOg* the plot revolves around an Orangeman who is hit on the head at the Sham Fight at Scarva on 13 July, and, to great humorous advantage, reaches a 'heaven' that is inhabited by Maeve, Cuchullain and Conchubar. The press comments printed in the programme for *Suzanne and the Sovereigns* reflect the readiness of the Ulster people to take this humour and to recognise and laugh at themselves.

> The play is an essay in humour of a genuinely intellectual character. . . . Neither Orangeman nor Nationalist with a spark of humour could help laughing consumedly as absurdity was heaped upon absurdity, till the climax was reached – Northern Whig.

> The authors have with a nimble wit and playful fancy hit upon the right spirit of burlesque. The proper note is struck in the first scene of the first act, and from that time onwards some extremely funny and clever skits are made. – News-Letter.

Set design for *Suzanne and the Sovereigns*
BELFAST CENTRAL LIBRARY

In May 1909, for their first season at the Grand Opera House, the Ulster Literary Theatre members chose *The Drone* and *The Troth* by Rutherford

Mayne, and *The Enthusiast* by Lewis Purcell. *The Drone* follows the story of two brothers, one an industrious County Down farmer, and the other a layabout who retreats to his den where he claims to be inventing a new fan bellows which will make the family's fortune. These popular plays had been regularly performed in Belfast by amateur groups but on this occasion an immediate difficulty arose with the Grand Opera House management. Traditionally the ULT had not given the real names of its cast and stage management, mostly because of their amateur status. The management of the Grand Opera House, on a basis of the professional approach, could not agree to this, and after a short wrangle the members of the company agreed to appear under their real names.

The *Nomad* appreciated equally the risk the ULT was running and the success of its outcome:

Some may have thought that to risk a whole week in such a huge place as the Grand Opera House was too ambitious an effort for such a youthful organisation but the operators of the Ulster Literary Theatre have been so characterised with extreme caution that those who have followed its footsteps were not at all surprised to learn that the faith of the Committee had been fully justified even before the doors were open on Monday evening and that the booking had at least stripped the experiment of any chance of financial failure. . . . gradually the eyes of the people are being opened. . . . never in the history of the Grand Opera House have the rafters rung with such genuine laughter as. . . . at the Drone. It was the hearty outburst of genuine hilarity as one realised that there was passing before the vision a series of realistic scenes such as anyone acquainted with rural Ulster must have witnessed. . . . reproduced with such amazing fidelity to detail.

A scene from *The Drone*, *c.* 1910, produced by the Ulster Literary Theatre
BELFAST CENTRAL LIBRARY

From 1909 to 1934, the Ulster Literary Theatre and later the Ulster Theatre performed regularly in the Grand Opera House, acting in plays written by Ulster men and women. In 1912, as well as the première of *Thompson in Tir-na-nOg*, they celebrated the work of Samuel Ferguson with a programme that included *The Drone*, *The Naming of Cuchullain* and music – 'Irish Airs, the Lark in the Clear Air, and the Lament for Thomas Davis'. In 1915, Helen Waddell wrote *The Spoiled Buddha*. In complete contrast to the realistic kitchen drama that had gone before, this was an esoteric symbolic drama in which 'the setting was very artistic and beautiful and the costumes were good and the acting was fearfully bad'. Year after year dramas, now forgotten, were produced. In 1918, George Morshiel, later known as George Shiels, wrote his first play for the Ulster Theatre. From 1921 he wrote regularly for the Abbey Theatre. His plays were always entertaining and attracted good houses, and though some directors thought them vulgar, they could not ignore the box office. Lennox Robinson felt that Shiels never ceased to be a dramatist of importance, considering that his unapologetic sentimentality set him in the tradition of Thomas Moore. He had something of a champion in Yeats, who described his work as 'rough, but good'. When Ernest Blythe asked if the Abbey could give Shiels a rest in 1935, Yeats refused, saying that it would be the equivalent of closing the doors.

The work of the Ulster Theatre continued to be presented at the Grand Opera House through the 1920s and the names of Charles Ayre and Richard Hayward were added to the list of writers, but by the 1930s it had petered out, and when both company and theatre lost money after the 1934 season of *The Schemer* by Thomas Kelly and *A Majority of One* by William Liddell, it was decided to end the relationship.

David Kennedy provides an important insight into the strengths and weaknesses of theatre in Northern Ireland:

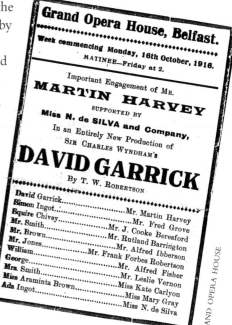

GRAND OPERA HOUSE

> It would be difficult, if not impossible to find in the history of Ulster another movement which attracted such a galaxy of talent and in which men and women of such diverse creeds and political views were united in a common purpose.
>
> The dispersion of these workers to Dublin, to London, and to New York was in the circumstances of the time inevitable, but it serves to indicate a fundamental flaw in the organisation of the Ulster Literary Theatre – it had no permanent home. A short season in the Opera House, Belfast, or in the Gaiety Theatre, Dublin; an occasional visit to Liverpool or London; a tour in the United States – while these won a wider public appreciation they were not enough to satisfy those Ulstermen who wished to make their professional careers in the theatre. . . . Had it not been for Rutherford Mayne and the Morrow family the Ulster Literary Theatre would not have survived the First World War. These men gave years of unselfish enthusiasm to it, and it is not intended to belittle their achievement in any way but if a theatre is to make a permanent mark on the culture of a country it must be a professional theatre in which writers, actors and producers can earn their livelihood.

The musical show *The Arcadians* —
'always merry and bright' — made several
return visits to the Grand Opera House;
these postcards accompanied the
1915 production.
GRAND OPERA HOUSE

4
FROM BURLESQUE TO BLACKOUT

Fred Warden's management of the Grand Opera House settled into an uncontroversial period after the change of name and purpose in 1909. The experiment of non-stop variety in the theatre does not seem to have been successful financially, as net profits for Warden Ltd of £4,516 in 1907 fell to £2,846 in 1908. In the years that followed, the programmes of the house covered a variety of tastes, with each year having its high and low points. Highlights were undoubtedly the visits of Sarah Bernhardt and of Martin Harvey and, at the other end of the cultural spectrum, a twice-nightly Hippodrome season in May and June gave popular performances of comedy, dancers, jumping cyclists, jugglers and acrobats under the stage management of J.G. Swanton.

The First World War had very little effect on the operation of the theatre, as touring companies were able to travel across the Irish Sea without restriction. However, the columns of the weekly newspaper, *Ireland's Saturday Night* (which gave good coverage to Grand Opera House productions) in the year 1917 reflect something of the attitudes of the Belfast public. The newspaper juxtaposes match reports with photographs of young soldiers under headings such as 'Football star succumbs' in which deaths in action are reported. Beside jaunty jingoistic cartoons are advertisements for concerts for blind and wounded colleagues by the 3rd Royal Inniskilling Fusiliers Band. Pictures of Belfast girls engaged in war work 'somewhere in Coventry' and 'photos found on various battlefields by Irish soldiers' are typical of the illustrations for the paper of the time.

The 1917 reviews of Grand Opera House shows, and indeed for all of the theatres, music-halls and picture houses in Belfast, are determinedly jolly. Throughout the first half of the year, a French farce regularly followed a musical or a hugely successful London comedy, such as *High Jinks*, *The Rotters*, *Mr Manhattan* or *Ye Gods*. But when D'Oyly Carte came to the theatre in April, the critic reported the absence of several popular voices missed by Belfast audiences:

> Leicester Tunks, for whom many friendly inquiries have been made, has joined up, and is undergoing aviation training. Sydney Granville, Walter Glynne, James Hay, Frank Steward, all prominent 'D'Oyly Carters' have transferred their energies to National needs and quite a number of the 'chorus boys' whose names don't appear in the programme have also joined up. Certain members of this company have

GREAT BRITAIN AND IRELAND, YOUR COUNTRY IS AT **WAR** WHAT ARE YOU DOING TO HELP HER?

If **you** cannot be a Soldier or a Nurse, your next duty is to help those that are now bearing the brunt of the battle, and you can do so by visiting the

GRAND OPERA HOUSE BELFAST

during the Week commencing September 14th, 1914, when the **Entire Receipts** will be handed over to the

Prince of Wales' National Relief Fund,

the **Ulster Theatre** giving its services free, and **Warden, Ltd.,** placing the Opera House, Staff, etc., at the disposal of the Fund.

By Permission of the Authors,

"If!" and **"Thompson in Tir-Na-N'og"**

The generous co-operation of the Public is invited to make this week a success.

Prices as usual.   Book Now.

GRAND OPERA HOUSE

Week commencing Monday, 23rd April, 1917.

D'Oyly Carte Repertory Co.

THIS EVENING—

THE MIKADO.

Written by W. S. GILBERT.

Composed by ARTHUR SULLIVAN.

The male members of this Company are either ineligible, exempted, or attested for the Army, or have been invalided out of the Army.

GRAND OPERA HOUSE

The Management would esteem it a favour if all **Ladies** would *remove their hats*, as it is obvious that the enjoyment of many is entirely spoilt by the view being obstructed by Ladies' Hats.

NEXT WEEK—May 19th.

The Sparkling Musical Play :

"The Officers' Mess."

From St. Martin's and the Prince's Theatres, London.

THEATRICAL GARDEN PARTY

IN AID OF THE

ACTORS' ORPHANAGE,

AT THE

ROYAL BOTANIC GARDENS, ::

:: :: REGENT'S PARK, N.W.,

On FRIDAY, MAY 30th, 1919.

All the Leading Actors and Actresses will 'assist.

TICKETS { 3s. each (before the day).
5s. ., (on the day).

Can be obtained at all the Theatres and Agencies.

The interior of the Grand Opera House during a performance of *The Royal Divorce* in 1916. Despite notices requesting that ladies remove their hats, most of the women in this audience are still wearing theirs, and some hats seem large enough to obscure the view. Before its restoration in 1980, the theatre held more than twice its present capacity.

GRAND OPERA HOUSE

now faced the Boer War, Sinn Fein troubles, Submarine scares and Zeppelin raids and still they are out to entertain the public.

The theatre took a long summer break in 1917, but returned with a showing of a moving picture, billed as a 'fairy film fantasy' starring the once 'divinely tall and most divinely fair' Annette Kellerman, the Australian nymph of 'world-wide aquatic fame'. Then Belfast audiences flocked to *Daddy Long Legs*, 'comic sensation of the season', *The Arcadians*, 'always merry and bright', *The Maid of the Mountains*, and *The Bing Boys*, 'the greatest of all music successes' billed as 'an excellent tonic for war-weariness'.

In September *Seven Days Leave*, a story of the war by Walter Howard, came to Belfast with a melodramatic plot of intrigue, passion and pathos, with an unfortunately unnamed local church choir taking part in the church scene. The local reviewer was impressed and added his own footnote:

> It would be a great mistake to assume it is a play only to entertain. It strikes a deeper note, for it correctly interprets the vast majority of Britishers. The centre of this plot is the presence in this country of German spies, who are masquerading as a wounded Belgian officer and his sister, whose husband was shot in defending that country from the invasion of the Teutons. It is a strong play superbly mounted.

Somerset Maugham's *The Land of Promise* was produced in the Grand Opera House in 1917.
GRAND OPERA HOUSE

Next came *The Land of Promise*, described as 'a Canadian play' by Somerset Maugham, which examined the woman's role in the new world – pioneer or domestic slave? But if Grand Opera House audiences felt stretched by the extremely topical question of the position of women, they were to be challenged further by the presentation of *Ghosts*. *Ireland's Saturday Night* approved of the production, and of the fact that the controversial play should be seen in Belfast, stating that 'the war has brought in its train a remarkable broadening of opinion on certain subjects which were previously tabooed'.

The average play-goer may not quite have realised the subject matter of the Ibsen drama before buying a ticket. The Grand Opera House had quite clearly stated that the production was 'For Adults Only', billing *Ghosts* as 'the play that was banned for 25 years', but this may in fact have raised false expectations. A week later a letter appeared in the paper from 'Bilfaust, Chewsday', written in thick Belfast dialect, reporting an alleged visit to the play. The writer records that she had just time to look at the decorations which must have cost a mint of money, and gold such as she had never seen in her born day, and enough plush curtain to make a carpet for Queen's Square, before the curtain went up:

> The furst thing A noticed on the stage was the flours. There was flours on the table, there was flours on the sideboord, there was flours on the mantle-boord, an there was a lauvely young girl watering the flours in the cornfern-ery, an' beautiful flours they wor too, an' barrin' the men an' weemin that wor actin in the play and wor ony earnin' their livin', the same flours wor the

only sweet an wholesum things connected way the whole show, so they wor.

The audience did the funniest things ye ivir saw. They laffed in the wrong places. They giggled at wha wor supposed to be the solemn places. They talked out loud and made remarks and didn't lissen hauf time. They cheered the most serious person in the play, the Parson, es if he wus the funny man. An' A believe in my heart what the majority av them wor waiting for wor the ghosts till appear ivery minnit, so A do.

During the twenties and thirties Belfast audiences had the opportunity of enjoying the great era of musicals such as *The Student Prince*, *Rose Marie*, *No, No, Nanette* and *The Desert Song*, whilst the plays of George Bernard Shaw were given by the Macdona Company. Shakespearean and classical drama continued to be provided by Sir Frank Benson, as well as by Charles Doran and his Shakespearean Company, and in this company young actors like Ralph Richardson and Donald Wolfit (Woolfitt) made early appearances on the Belfast stage in minor roles. During a visit in 1923, Wolfit and Hilton Edwards were listed in the programme both as members of the cast and as stage managers.

The year 1928 provided a typically varied bill of fare for Belfast audiences. At the start of the year, Charles Doran brought *The Cardinal*; notices encouraging school parties advised that 'Parents especially should read the announcements about facilities for children attending the plays and urge these on the teachers'. This play was followed by *The Student Prince* with full London company direct from His Majesty's Theatre. From February to April, audiences enjoyed a selection of touring plays that included *The Ghost Train*, a 'sensational mystery play', *My Son John*, a musical comedy, *The Co-optimists*, a 'pierrotic entertainment' and *Good Morning Bill* by P.G. Wodehouse. Then in May, after an absence of ten years, the Abbey Theatre returned and for the first time Belfast audiences were able to see a staging of a Sean O'Casey play when *Juno and the Paycock* was presented with George Shiels's *Professor Tim*. *Ireland's Saturday Night* was enthusiastic about the visit:

The talented Abbey Players had a wonderful week at Belfast Opera House. 'Professor Tim' played to capacity during Monday, Tuesday and Wednesday, while 'Juno and the Paycock' drew more people to Great Victoria Street than would have filled six houses of the same size and still left a disappointed queue. We must have them back again and soon.

The Abbey Theatre was followed by the Popular Opera Company which gave a selection of well-known works, and then the Macdona Company arrived with plays by George Bernard Shaw. The company was brave enough to present the whole six hours of *Man and Superman* including *Don Juan in Hell* in a performance that began at 5.30 p.m. and offered a mere

GRAND OPERA HOUSE, BELFAST.

Week commencing Monday, Feb. 26th, 1923.
MATINEES—WEDNESDAY and FRIDAY at 2.

MR. CHARLES DORAN
and his Shakespearean Company.

THIS EVENING:
SHAKESPEARE'S TRAGEDY—
OTHELLO.

Duke of Venice......................Norman F. Shelley
Brabantio, a Senator..................Francis L. Sullivan
Gratiano, Brother to Brabantio........Abraham Sofaer
Lodovico, Kinsman to Brabantio........Cecil Parker
Othello, a Noble Moor, in the service of the
    Venetian State......................CHARLES DORAN
Cassio, his Lieutenant..................Ralph Richardson
Iago, his Ancient..................W. Earle Grey
Roderigo, a Venetian Gentleman......Christian Morrow
Montano, Othello's Predecessor in the Govern-
    ment of Cyprus..................Horace Wentworth
Desdemona, Daughter to Brabantio and Wife
    to Othello..................Barbara Everest
Emilia, Wife to Iago..................Irene Marston
Bianca, Mistress to Cassio..................Muriel Hutchinson

Sailors, Officers, Gentlemen, Messengers,
Musicians, Heralds, and Attendants.

GENTLEMEN can enjoy a Cigarette with their Cup of Coffee, in luxurious comfort, in the CARLTON, Donegall Place.

Charles Doran's company was a sound training ground for Shakespearean actors. On a visit in 1923, Ralph Richardson, Hilton Edwards and Donald Wolfit were in the cast and Wolfit and Edwards doubled as assistant stage managers.
GRAND OPERA HOUSE

half-hour interval for refreshments. Booking for this epic was described as 'heavy'.

After the summer break, the theatre reopened with a return visit of Seymour Hicks in his 'funniest play', *Mr What's-his-name*, which he directed himself and which had just come back from a Canadian tour. Later in the autumn the comedy *Oh Kay!* came to the Grand Opera House. *Ireland's Saturday Night* recorded some of the aphorisms:

> A woman's place is in the house? – No, a woman's place is in the channel.
> Milkmen seldom get married. They see women too early in the morning.
> She was a good cook as cooks go and like all good cooks – she went.
> The comedian, producing an empty beer box, described it as a hopeless case.
> Altogether, Oh Kay! proved a show.

During this period only minor changes were made to the running of the theatre. A cast-iron and glass canopy was extended at the front of the house in 1913, and dressing-room accommodation was added over the open yard. In the 1920s a long-standing argument about whether it was permissible to smoke in the theatre reached the compromise of banning pipes from the stalls or the circle, but allowing their use in the cramped and hot confines of the gods, and by 1930, programmes bore the 'urgent request' to patrons to refrain from smoking pipes in the stalls, circle or boxes.

But in 1926, a more significant note appeared for the first time in Grand Opera House programmes, heralding the coming of a new age in entertainment: 'The Royal Cinema, Arthur Square, the Centre of Cinematic Art, Continuous from 2 till 10.30. Prices (including tax) Before 5pm 9d & 1/3. After 5pm 1/3 & 2/-.' Three years before his death, Fred Warden had embraced the exciting and expanding world of the moving picture show, and had entered into the cinema business.

Edward Buckley, who succeeded Fred Warden as managing director in 1929
GRAND OPERA HOUSE

After Fred Warden's death, Edward Buckley took over as managing director, assisted by James McCann, who had been resident manager and secretary. When McCann died in 1937, he was replaced by Miss Bolton, who is still vividly remembered as a powerful force at the Grand Opera House. Under Buckley's guidance the theatre continued to flourish. Improvements were made to the stalls entrance in Glengall Street, and the oak panelling was added. It may have been around this time that the dressing rooms were identified by the names of cities. Those who remember them recall that the closer you were to *London* the higher was your prestige, so the dressing room called *Leeds* was quite a shabby area. Edward Buckley made no startling changes to the artistic policy of the theatre, continuing to welcome the amateurs of Northern Ireland to its stage and bringing the favourite touring companies, as well as new stars and famous artistes. He followed the fashion of the new and retained the best of the old, and the prestige of the theatre was rewarded in 1934 when the Duke of Gloucester attended a Command Performance of *The Lady of the Camellias*, with Jean Forbes-Robertson in the leading role.

The newspapers relished every detail of the splendid night. This review was typical:

The Grand Opera House last night was gaily decorated with flags and bunting and a centrepiece in front of the building showed a large painting of His Royal Highness, the Duke of Gloucester, with the word 'Welcome' emblazoned underneath. . . . outside the theatre large crowds had collected long before the hour for the performance to start. Throughout the evening these crowds did not lessen at all until the Royal Visitor had taken his departure. . . . Never had the theatre looked so well. The entrance hall was banked with hydrangeas among which glowing geraniums made a delightful harmony. The front of the Royal Box was covered with crimson carnations in the centre of which was an ensign bearing the Royal arms. Overhead was an arch of crimson and white carnations. The fronts of the other boxes were similarly treated. Women were wearing their smartest frocks . . . jewels, especially diamonds, were much in evidence. They winked and flashed on every side. Smart naval and military uniforms, some of the latter in scarlet and others in green, mingled with the lovely frocks and jewels.

Everyone arrived early. At first there was a continuous ripple of laughter and conversation. Then a hush of expectancy settled on the house . . . the orchestra struck up the National Anthem and the vast audience rose. . . . Then very quietly and without any ostentation the Duke of Gloucester appeared in the Royal Box, with him the Governor and the Duke of Abercorn. Then the National Anthem was taken up by the audience and sung with a heartiness that could not have failed to impress the King's son. This was followed by a storm of applause that reverberated through the building and out to the waiting crowds on the street.

During the long interval the Duke of Gloucester sent for Miss Jean Forbes-Robertson, and congratulated her upon her performance. He hoped, he said, that if she were not too tired she would accompany him to the dance which he was going to at the Royal Belfast Golf Club.

Jean Forbes-Robertson was popular not only with royalty but with Belfast audiences, and later that year she brought to the theatre her everlasting *Peter Pan*, a show that never seemed to grow up and for which she is probably chiefly remembered. After the final performance, as was the custom, she made a short speech. She said she was delighted to be in this beautiful city, and thanked the audience for giving her such a reception. 'Never had they had one like it.'

But for sheer weight of popularity, nothing in the thirties surpassed the waves of enthusiasm that met the visit of the great favourite of the day, Gracie Fields, on 18 September 1933. The *Belfast Telegraph* reported that at five o'clock the queue itself was 'a unique event', by 6.30 the theatre was filled to capacity, 'not one part but every area, and the audience represented every section, from those on the higher levels to the patrons of the stalls and circle'. The report stated that the welcome accorded to Gracie Fields was 'such that might be given to the greatest of personages'.

Gracie Fields came to Belfast at a time when variety was the preferred diet of theatre-goers, and throughout the thirties the Grand Opera House

1930s Grand Opera House programme cover
GRAND OPERA HOUSE

Commencing Tuesday, Feb. 20th, 1934, at 7-30.
Matinees : Wednesday, Thursday, Friday & Saturday at 2.

THE DANIEL MAYER COMPANY present
JEAN FORBES-ROBERTSON
IN
PETER PAN
By J. M. BARRIE

Cast and Production direct from London Palladium Season.

Peter Pan	Jean Forbes-Robertson
Captain James Hook	Lionel Gadsden
Mr. Darling	J. Courtland
Mrs. Darling	Rosemary Bamber
Wendy Moira Angela Darling	Edith Joyce
John Napoleon Darling	Michael Goodwin
Michael Nicholas Darling	Arthur West Payne
Nana	George Elliston
Tinker Bell	Jenny Wren
Tootles	Andre Carter
Nibs	Dudley Hamilton
Slightly	W. G. Manning
Curley	Geo. Hart
First Twin	Stanley Bridger
Second Twin	Douglas Beaumont
Smee	Cecil Fowler
Gentleman Starkey	Frank Elton
Cookson	George Hudson
Mullins	Carl Wright
Cecco	James Willoughby
Jukes	Frederick Page
Noodler	J. Courtland
First Pirate	W. Kirby
Second Pirate	Arthur J. Franks
Black Pirate	Sam Henry

PHONE 4595
Belfast GOLF SCHOOL
A BOON TO BEGINNERS.
Learn to play Golf.
NOTICE TO GOLFERS—Improve your weak strokes under the expert guidance of L. FORSHAW, late professional of the Lisburn Golf Club. We stock everything for the Golfers at the keenest prices. Clubs made on the premises.

Individual Tuition costs only 2/- per half-hour.   Make an Appointment by Phone 4595
17 COLLEGE STREET, BELFAST.

GRAND OPERA HOUSE

Sir Frank Benson faithfully brought his Shakespearean Company to Belfast every January; he finally made two farewell tours in 1930 and 1931.

GRAND OPERA HOUSE

Matheson Lang, who made a successful visit to the Grand Opera House in 1935

THEATRE MUSEUM, V. & A.

management followed the trend. Carl Rosa continued to come, and after an uncertain period enjoyed a renewal of enthusiasm in 1934, with a full house for *Die Fledermaus*, for what was probably its first performance in Belfast, and for *Faust*, which included a ballet, where 'the attendance was good . . . which gives grounds for the hope that opera may experience a return to something like the former favour which it enjoyed in the city'. When the Ballet Russe de Paris came in 1935, it performed before a large and appreciative audience.

In 1930 Sir Frank Benson, already over seventy years old, announced his farewell tour. He visited Belfast in January with a repertoire that included *As You Like It* and *The Merchant of Venice*. In 1931, he again announced his farewell tour. This time he visited the Grand Opera House with *A Midsummer Night's Dream*.

Throughout the thirties plays of good quality and contemporary interest were presented. The Abbey Theatre continued to bring first-class productions, and occasionally a popular full-length play such as *Ten Minute Alibi* or *The Late Christopher Bean* transferred from London. A few provincial repertory theatres sent productions on tour: in 1930 Barry Jackson of Birmingham Repertory Theatre brought a production of *The Apple Cart* by George Bernard Shaw, a year after its première. *Bitter Sweet*, Noël Coward's most popular musical, came direct from His Majesty's Theatre, London, in 1931, two years after it had opened, and J.B. Priestley's *The Good Companions* came to Belfast within a year of its opening, in 1932. The dramatic event of the season of 1935 was a personal visit by Matheson Lang in his new play, *There Go All of Us*. Ruth Draper made a celebrated visit in 1932, but contrary to popular tradition Anna Pavlova did not, though the company recalling her name (which she had founded in 1911) came in 1931, shortly after her death.

But apart from a few notable exceptions, the vast majority of twice-nightly programmes presented a happy blend of music and laughter. The shows immediately preceding the visit of Gracie Fields included such varied acts and artistes as the Debonair Bell Boys, the Gipsy Girls Band, the Inebriated Gentleman and Mamie Souter, the Modern Bunch of Mirth.

On 3 December, a twice-nightly variety programme headed by Eddie May and his Hollywood Masquerades included 'the BBC star Annette, Radio's Latest Success'. Further down the bill the names of Lew Grade and Marjorie Pointer appeared; they were described as 'the electric sparks, superb dancing'. For Lew Grade at that time, the life of a touring variety artiste was always precarious, fraught with financial problems. In Belfast the houses were good, but not good enough to cover their expenses.

In the same period Jack Hylton came with his big band, and so did Jack Doyle, 'the Coming Heavy Weight Champion of the World', who sang Irish songs and gave an exhibition of skipping and shadow boxing.

A week after the excitement of Gracie Fields's visit, the circus came to town. Chapman's Great Continental Zoo and Circus, 'the greatest aggregation of performing animals ever presented on any stage', was no tame affair: shown in a large steel arena were real wild animals, and the circus acts included ponies, 'Black Bear Comedy, Boomerang the boxing kangaroo, Musical Comedy Elephants, Performing Polar Bears and Forest Bred Lions'.

The year of 1934 was eventful. In addition to the important visit of the Duke of Gloucester, the programme included popular shows like the music-hall legend Will Fyffe, of whom Sir John Gielgud said, he 'excelled at mimicry and strange transformations, and I was never sure whether I would recognise [him] from one number to the next'. There were many undemanding entertainments such as *Sporting Love* – 'Lovely Girls, Haunting Tunes, Packed with Laughs' – which attracted large audiences. Some strange pairings appeared on programmes. In May, 'Neddy the Lovable Donkey' appeared on the same bill along with a selection from *The Mikado*.

It was a year in which disaster almost struck the theatre. One of the most prestigious and, no doubt, expensive shows of the time had been secured. The very popular show *The White Horse Inn* had come as an entire

Jack Doyle, 'the coming heavyweight champion of the world', who sang Irish songs and gave an exhibition of skipping and shadow-boxing, photographed at the stage door in the early 1930s
PUBLIC RECORD OFFICE OF NORTHERN IRELAND

NOVEMBER, 1932

The PICTURE HOUSE
ROYAL AVENUE

The House of Perfect Sound

C. F. O'DOWDA, MANAGER.

In the late 1920s the advent of the 'talkies' made a real impact on the entertainment possibilities for Belfast's citizens. But earlier Fred Warden had entered the world of moving pictures and was advertising the Royal Cinema, Arthur Square, in Grand Opera House programmes.
LINEN HALL LIBRARY

Grand Opera House, Belfast.
Week Commencing Monday, March 15th.
J. Bannister Howard's Co.
From the GAIETY THEATRE, LONDON.

THE GIRL ON THE FILM

MATINEE, Friday.   Time and Prices as usual.

Picture palace meets the theatre
GRAND OPERA HOUSE

production from the London Coliseum; it had been described as 'the biggest show that was ever presented in the city', and it had run only a few nights when a fire broke out. The *Belfast News-Letter* covered the story.

A fire which broke out at the Grand Opera House yesterday morning did considerable damage to the gallery and roof before it was subdued by the City Fire Brigade. The outbreak was discovered by a police constable shortly before 7 o'clock. When the Brigade under Chief Officer Smith arrived, smoke was issuing from almost every window. . . . sawdust and tarpaulin sheets were spread over the floor and seats in the circle and stalls, and this substantially reduced the damage that might have been caused by the water. The flames had spread through the ventilators to the roof and were rapidly consuming the gallery but in half an hour they were extinguished thanks to particularly smart work on the part of the firemen.

In consequence of the fire there was no presentation of the musical comedy *The White Horse Inn* last night, but steps were immediately taken towards the resumption of the performance tonight. It is believed that the outbreak was caused by a burning cigarette end thrown down by someone in the crowded gallery on Tuesday night.

Mr James McCann, the general manager of the Grand Opera House, told the *Belfast News-Letter*, 'It is a deplorable thing, especially in view of the great popularity of the musical comedy which is being presented, but we hope to resume on Thursday evening.' This they did but takings were reduced by the fact that the gallery could not be reopened.

With characteristic enterprise, the management of the Grand Opera House decided to take advantage of the opportunity this difficulty offered. On 2 August 1934 the *Belfast Telegraph* reported that the theatre would be reopened in a much-improved condition. James McCann had decided that this was an opportune time to replace the stage which, it was felt, had become obsolete, to create adequate accommodation for a big show like *The White Horse Inn*, and to 'effect economy in the transport and housing of the scenic effects which are an essential part of the theatre's paraphernalia'. The architects Messrs Stevenson & Sons and the contractors H. & J. Martin carried out the work in two months, and the result, by which the stage, now finished in maple wood, could be lifted in sections, to allow scenery to be stored below, according to the theatre management made a 'stage which will now be on a par with the finest in the kingdom'.

The gallery has been entirely renovated and patrons will find their seats upholstered in repp of a light and pleasing texture, and in an equally and satisfying style of linoleum. The auditorium has been redecorated and presents a colourful and luxurious aspect. In other respects the interior beauty of the theatre has been enhanced, and no detail has been overlooked to establish the Opera House on a pedestal worthy of its traditions, and of [the] capital city.

Those who remember going to the Grand Opera House during the 1930s and after the Second World War recall the atmosphere in the gods.

The early door system was still in operation, and patrons of the gallery (who unless they had gained a seat in the front row would have their knees in somebody's back, and somebody's knees in their back) would amuse themselves in the wait before the curtain rose or the conductor came out for the overture. Ukuleles would appear, and the waiting audience would join in songs from the shows in anticipation of the real thing. Balloons would be blown up and floated down to the stalls and circle. Balloons would be blown up and burst. On one occasion the din grew too much for the long-suffering leader of the Grand Opera House orchestra, Samuel Swanton, and James McCann was sent up to try to reduce the noise. The chief culprit turned out to be a respectable gentleman, a buyer for the Bank Buildings department store, who was happily blowing up balloons for his children. When it was pointed out to him that his behaviour might be a distraction to the orchestra, he is said to have replied, 'Sure all the drums in Scarva couldn't put Sam Swanton's orchestra off. They're playing the same tunes they were playing in the Alhambra twenty years ago!'

If a gentleman arrived in the more expensive seats with a hard hat on, the cry would rise up 'Hard hat! Hard hat! Take it off! Take it off!' followed by a huge cheer when that item of headgear was removed. It was all great fun, and apparently was the preliminary to all types of entertainment, even the ballet, after the Second World War; it meant that the audience was well warmed up, and would greet the start of the show with real enthusiasm.

In 1980, Norman Ballantine of the *News Letter* remembered the 1930s tradition of going to a variety show on St Patrick's Day:

> In a way I suppose my late childhood and early adulthood coincided with the very best years of the Grand Opera House. Every St Patrick's Day we would crowd the terraces of Ravenhill for the Schools' Cup final, and in the evening would gallop up miles of stone steps to the gods in the Opera house for a variety show in which the comedians were all primed as to the local importance of the day and came out with corny jokes about Methody and Inst and we all roared and clapped and stamped our feet and threw balloons down on to the stage, and sometimes pennies if the jokes were particularly corny.

In the 1930s, despite the economic depression, the theatre continued in a confident and buoyant mood, offering shows that specialised in determined gaiety. In March 1935 Sir Harry Lauder performed to a large and enthusiastic audience. It was felt by many that although Lauder's voice was not so sonorous as of old, he still retained all his magic personality along with the repertoire he had made so famous: from 'Oh, it's nice to get up in the mornin' but it's nicer to stay in bed', 'Roamin' in the gloamin'' and 'I love a lassie' to 'Keep right on to the end of the road'. And

> Just a wee deoch an dorus
> Before we gang awa' . . .
> If ye can say
> It's a braw, bricht moonlicht nicht
> Yer a' richt, that's a'.

Harry Lauder, the Scottish music-hall artiste, who came to the Grand Opera House in twice-nightly variety in 1935
THEATRE MUSEUM, V. & A.

Jack Payne's Big Band, one of the
many big bands who came to the
Grand Opera House in the 1930s
PUBLIC RECORD OFFICE OF
NORTHERN IRELAND

Layton and Johnstone appeared in a variety programme that included jugglers and football on bicycles, while the novelty acts included Mademoiselle Veronica, 'the girl with £2,000 legs, the champion High Kicker of the World with her French Blondes'. Big bands were represented by Mrs Jack Hylton, Jack Payne and Henry Hall and his Orchestra, 'the idol of radio millions!' Several other shows claimed their celebrity from the airwaves. *In Town Tonight* featured Toni Rice and his BBC Band. Of the depression there were few indications, except perhaps the insistence on merriment and escapism. Only when the Bangor Unemployed Men took part in the Eighth Northern Dramatic Feis in 1936 in the Grand Opera House was there a hint that there might be economic problems in Northern Ireland.

In October 1935 a show called *Hail Prosperity* came to Belfast. It was described as a revue, but of such a harmless nature that you could 'Bring your children, you will hear nothing offensive. Good clean comedy is our aim.' The show boasted 900 beautiful dresses, 28 scenes of comedy and splendour, a cast of over 60 artistes, and 'no jokes that you have heard before'. The accompanying *Belfast Prosperity Bulletin* contains a few contemporary references and an idea of the humour in store for the audience.

Hail Prosperity – a defiantly optimistic
and lavish revue staged in 1935, a year in
which Belfast continued to experience
the worst of the depression and the 'wee
yard' of shipbuilders Workman Clark
was forced to close down.
GRAND OPERA HOUSE

Early this year, the Theatrical world was startled by the production of 'Hail Prosperity'. Almost simultaneously the Premier announced that Britain had entered a period of unexampled prosperity. Whilst we are too modest to claim a connection between the two occurrences, we would point out that the coincidence is significant.

Judging by our own experience of the last few months, we can safely confirm the optimistic remarks of our late Prime Minister, and hasten to pass on a message of hope and confidence to those industries who have felt a draught these last few years.

Our sympathy goes to the widow of the man, who at a Communist meeting, raised his right hand to draw the speaker's attention.

This bronzed handsome man is Signor Forani. Pretend not to notice his abstract manner. He has just passed through a terrible ordeal. Whilst visiting his native country during the vacation, he was stricken with rheumatism in his right arm, and he had a terrible job persuading the gendarmeri to believe him when they demanded to know why his arm was not raised in a Fascist salute when Mussolini passed. The strain has left its mark upon him.

The shadow of Fascism, which was a subject for laughter in 1935, passed over Belfast in 1939, when war was declared. Until 1940, nothing much changed at the Grand Opera House. In October 1939, Jimmy O'Dea played twice nightly, in *O'D Revels of 1939*, and in 1940 the Royal Carl Rosa Opera Company made a visit.

In 1939 there was the first tour by Hilton Edwards and Micheál Mac Liammóir, who continued to bring the productions of Dublin's Gate Theatre to Belfast for many years as they made their significant contribution to Irish touring theatre. Edwards and Mac Liammóir had engaged an exotic-looking, charming, efficient and multilingual woman called Toska Bissing to handle their press contacts and take small roles. In his biography *The Boys*, Christopher Fitz-Simon records Hilton Edwards's initial misgivings on crossing the border on their visit to Belfast, which was to be fitted in between Cork and an ambitious tour to Belgrade:

Toska Bissing organised a backstage party for the press after a performance of *Death Takes a Holiday*. The novelty of the idea pleased the theatre correspondents, particularly Nuala Moran of The Leader. . . . She wrote that 'Hilton Edwards was forced to take the pipe out of his mouth, leave his maps down and say something' – which he then did at some length. During the informal question period, when the possibility of war was being discussed, he flippantly asked her if she would prefer to be shot in Belfast or Belgrade, and she voted for Belgrade because she had been to Belfast and would like to see somewhere else before she died. Hilton said he never really believed the Balkans existed outside novels. 'Remote and impenetrable as the Balkans appear from Dublin,' he continued, 'it is easier to get into Bulgaria than across the frontier of the six counties at the top of our own map.' . . . After the fall of curtain on 19 January, the final night of the Dublin season, Micheál Mac Liammóir came forward to thank the audience. He also thanked the actors, and said they were all looking forward to Cork – he did not mention Belfast – and, 'weather and war permitting, we shall make a European tour'.

GRAND OPERA HOUSE

The Belfast visit was a great success, aided by the effective work of Toska Bissing, and full houses enjoyed *Wuthering Heights* and *And So to Bed*. Mac Liammóir had decided against Shakespeare, because Wolfit had presented a Shakespeare repertoire recently in the Grand Opera House. The final production of the week was *Night Must Fall*, but as if to prove Edwards's theory of the impenetrability of the North correct, the company was left without a set on the morning of the Friday. By the afternoon, customs officials released the sets, and after frantic efforts by crew and cast alike the set was erected and the show went ahead.

The Grand Opera House during the
Second World War, with the Savoy
Players, a temporary wartime repertory
company, advertised on the hoarding
ULSTER FOLK AND TRANSPORT MUSEUM

The Gate continued to make annual visits to the Grand Opera House. But in 1940, restrictions were placed on the travel of theatre companies within Britain and, to his great credit, Edward Buckley stepped in and formed a repertory company from actors who were playing in Ireland. This was the first and last time that the Grand Opera House had its own repertory company for any lengthy period.

The Savoy Players, as they were known, made an immense contribution to wartime Belfast. Night after night, with two performances on Saturday at 6.15 and 8.30, week after week, with a short break in the summer, they played to full houses. Frederick Tripp was producer, Henry Peirse was scenic artist, and Dudley Hare led the musical sextet, a musical luxury not enjoyed by many repertory theatres of the time. The original company included Norman Cidgey, Frederick Victor, Ian Priestley Mitchell, Jack Garvey, David Russell, Evelyn Kerry, Margery Weston, Peggy O'Dare, June Daunt and Hazel Grey. Later, actors were replaced by others including Basil Lord, Guy Rolfe, Jane Aird, Coralie Carmichael and James Young. Of the company some, like Coralie Carmichael, were drafted in from the Gate Theatre; others, like Basil Lord, went on to make it in the movies, and only Norman Cidgey remained from start to finish. It was estimated that this backbone member of the company studied 30 pages a week, or 1,560 pages a year, or 7,800 pages for the span of the company.

The Savoy Players specialised in plays by contemporary writers, and throughout the war the works of Noël Coward, John Galsworthy, George Bernard Shaw, Frederick Lonsdale and Terence Rattigan were regularly shown. These actors could equally easily turn their hand to a Ben Travers farce or an Agatha Christie thriller. Fred Tripp had mounted several pantomimes in Belfast before the war, but he chose the plays for the Savoy company very cleverly. He tailored his repertoire skilfully to match the talents of his cast, avoiding the over-ambitious, and, because his original cast at least was English, he refused to bow to demands for the production of Irish plays. He worked out a system of choosing four plays at a time, so that censorship requirements and costumes could be organised together. Rehearsals would begin on a Tuesday to open the following Monday. Occasionally the success of a play would justify an extra week, and it is not surprising that often plays with a topical or patriotic theme, such as *This Happy Breed*, by Noël Coward, *To Dream Again*, by Veronica Haigh (much of which was written in an air raid shelter), and *Watch on the Rhine*, by Lillian Hellman, were very popular. A farce called *Is Your Honeymoon Really Necessary?* also earned an extended run. Fred Tripp himself felt that his best productions included *Jane Eyre*, *The Importance of Being Earnest*, *The Man Who Came To Dinner*, *Ten Little Niggers*, *Madame Conte*, *Dear Brutus*, *Uncle Harry*, *Blithe Spirit* and *Mary Rose*.

Jimmy Dugan, who was commissionaire at the gallery door from 1896 until after the Second World War, recalled how the shows at the Grand Opera House carried on, even during the blitz:

> I got blew out of my house and went to the country for a while, but I come up every night. There was nights here at that time when there'd be only half a dozen in the gallery. Sometimes there'd only be one or two so we'd move them down to the pit, and I'd go home.

This keeper of the gallery felt that the war had one benefit – queues:

> People's different now – they're civilised. Between you and me, I think the blitz did them a lot of good. They let ye walk up the stairs in front of them now. . . . I've seen the crowd coming up there like a riot. I've seen nearly 1,700 in that gallery. In the old days there was no queues, you know. They all came in with a rush. Many's the time I was put on my back when I opened the door down below.

An American war correspondent wrote in the *Belfast Telegraph*, at a time when the Savoy company was about to present its two-hundredth play, as follows:

> These players, all of them, are very firmly a part of Belfast, so thoroughly a part of the entertainment life of the city that they are known and loved by thousands of servicemen of all the Allied Nations. Few members of the entertainment world are doing more than they are doing right here. I have seen many plays in London, Los Angeles, New York. In no city or theatre have I seen players so warmly received. . . . Yes, when I return to far-off Los Angeles in America, like so many who have visited Belfast and the theatre here, there will go with me an unfading memory of the many very pleasant performances I have seen.

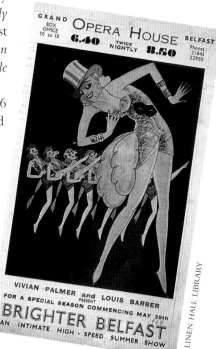

Irving Berlin's *This Is the Army* was
enormously popular when it came to
Belfast in 1944.

PUBLIC RECORD OFFICE OF NORTHERN IRELAND

However good the standards of the Savoy Players were, their productions
were eclipsed in 1944, when for three weeks the United States Army presented *This Is the Army* to audiences at the Grand Opera House of 30,000.
Enthusiasm reached fever pitch when Irving Berlin made a personal
appearance in Belfast. A year later General Dwight Eisenhower came to the
theatre to see *The Lady from Edinburgh*, which the Savoy Players had revived
especially for his benefit, when he became a freeman of the city of Belfast.
And the pattern of entertaining new freemen was repeated several weeks
later when Field Marshal Sir Bernard Montgomery was present at *This
Happy Breed*, and when the distinguished Ulster soldiers Field Marshal Sir
Alan Brooke and Field Marshal Sir Harold Alexander were in the audience
for *Hay Fever*.

Writing in 1980, *News Letter* columnist Norman Ballantine remembered
one of these gala occasions:

> In the good old days of the Grand Opera House you went in, if you were
> looking for the best seats, by a door on the corner of Glengall Street (now
> permanently bricked up and I don't know why) and were in a small, cosy
> foyer with a gracefully curving staircase of white marble, covered with red
> carpet, going up to the carpeted foyer behind the dress circle where the cour-
> teous ushers paraded in the uniform of field marshals, and where I almost
> mistook Field Marshal Viscount Alexander for an usher when he was over

here on an official visit with Field Marshal Sir Alan Brooke to a gala show in the good old Opera House.

In the immediate post-war euphoria it was a gala night of quality that just can't happen nowadays (and possibly never again, more's the pity). Cabinet Ministers, Lord Mayors and all sorts of VIPs were there in droves and Lady Brookeborough came to the show even though she was suffering from a severe back ailment.

A colleague with the Irish Times, my very good friend the late Jimmy Boyd, was telephoning a blow by blow account of this august occasion to his newspaper when he mentioned that Lady Brookeborough, partly encased in plaster of Paris, was carried into a box on a stretcher, the copytaker at the other end interrupted him with: 'Would you repeat the bit about the Prime Minister's wife being plastered in Paris.'

The war was over and a new era of hope and enthusiasm had arrived.

General Dwight Eisenhower is presented to members of the Savoy Players during his visit to a gala performance in 1945. On his right is Edward Buckley, managing director, on his left, Miss Bolton, company secretary.
PUBLIC RECORD OFFICE OF NORTHERN IRELAND

Doings of Larry O'Hooligan

"Well done, Ike! It's largely owing to you that we in Ulster are still free men"

Ireland's Saturday Night's Larry O'Hooligan meets General Eisenhower, 1945
IRELAND'S SATURDAY NIGHT

Members of the Sadler's Wells Opera Company with Grand Opera House staff during their visit in 1945. James Johnston, the famous tenor, is on the right of the front row.
PUBLIC RECORD OFFICE OF NORTHERN IRELAND

5

'IN ASSOCIATION WITH CEMA . . .'

THE WAVE OF OPTIMISM that swept the UK in the immediate after-math of the Second World War was highlighted in Belfast by a three-week visit by Sadler's Wells Opera Company to the Grand Opera House in the summer of 1945; despite a heatwave every seat in the theatre was taken for every performance, in which *Così fan tutte*, *The Bartered Bride* and *Madame Butterfly* were given, by casts which included Joan Cross and Peter Pears. The mastermind behind the visit, and behind much that was positive in the arts in the decade that followed, was Tyrone Guthrie. Guthrie had been born at Tunbridge Wells in Kent, but he accomplished so much for the province and was associated so strongly with it that he is regarded as an honorary Ulsterman, and was always enormously proud of his connections with that part of the world. A great-grandson of the nineteenth-century actor Tyrone Power, who had another famous actor great-grandson, who bore his name but outstripped him in fame, Guthrie first came to Belfast in 1928 as one of the earliest producers of the BBC, but after periods at the Scottish National Theatre Society, the BBC in London and the Festival Theatre, Cambridge, he joined the Old Vic as producer in 1933. The Old Vic was then under the control of Lilian Baylis,

Opposite:
Tyrone Guthrie, who had such an impact on postwar productions at the Grand Opera House, first came to Belfast in 1928 as a BBC producer. He is seen here in white shirt and bow-tie taking a BBC rehearsal off Linenhall Street.
ULSTER MUSEUM

Jimmy Dugan, doorman at the Grand
Opera House and keeper of the gods
from 1896 to 1945
IRELAND'S SATURDAY NIGHT

who had achieved the remarkable feat of presenting the entire Shakespearean cycle. When Tyrone Guthrie arrived he introduced distinguished guest artistes, raised production values and turned round the finances of the company. After the death of Miss Baylis he became director of drama and later administrator of both the Old Vic and Sadler's Wells companies, which Miss Baylis had acquired.

So it was from this position of influence that he persuaded the prestigious opera company to make its first visit. The precursor of the Arts Council, the Council for the Encouragement of Music and the Arts, or CEMA, worked with Guthrie to make the visit a success. A leading figure in CEMA was the playwright Jack Loudan, and he was assisted by Betty Lowry, who later went on to become drama critic and woman's editor of the *Belfast Telegraph*. She vividly remembers the excitement that first visit generated and some of the problems involved. Careful arrangements had been made with the legendary theatrical landladies who ran digs for visiting companies in Joy Street. However, when the staff of CEMA escorted the Sadler's Wells members to these rooms, chaos ensued. Rooms that had been confirmed by letter were occupied or did not exist, and Betty Lowry finished by bringing a principal singer home to her mother's house in Bangor, to her mother's surprise and subsequent delight.

Stories about these theatrical digs abound. Joy Street used to be known as the Street of the Three Ps, representing Pride, Poverty and Pianos, because each house had a piano for the use of visiting artistes. Charlie Chaplin stayed in Number 24 in 1906 and 1907. At about the same time one occupant of the street, Mary McGreavy, was keeping cows in the back yard; another, Madame Lura, gained a living by reading palms and crystal balls. In Cromac Street, round the corner, Aggie Toner had a shop, not exactly a second-hand clothes shop, but one where theatrical clothes, or clothes that actresses might wear, might be had. It was a good place to glean information about visiting companies, and somewhere where an enterprising, stylish Belfast woman might pick up something a little out of the ordinary. On one famous occasion Athol Street was flooded, and the marooned artistes were unable to reach the theatre. To make matters worse, they ran short of food, and supplies had to be hoisted to the upstairs rooms to the delight of a cheering crowd.

For the visit of Sadler's Wells, Betty Lowry remembers drama of a different kind. Their tour coincided with the famous general election of 1945. In a café off Linenhall Street members of the company crowded round the radio to hear the results come in. Cheer after cheer rose up as Labour victory followed Labour victory.

This first visit to Belfast of the distinguished opera company attracted a lot of attention. 'W' of *Ireland's Saturday Night* went backstage at the Grand Opera House and spoke to the wardrobe mistress who was ensconced high up under the roof, with all the skips of costumes required to tour four operas. The 62 skips held about 500 costumes, and about 150 wigs, and all the linens had to be laundered between performances. The company came with its own portable offices, and with 26 tons of electrical equipment as well as sets and its own orchestra. 'W' had a good time delving into the corners of the theatre.

Here's the dressing room. Last night's costumes still hung round the wall . . . the mirrors in the room were autographed in red make-up: Winifred, Jean, Mollie, Olwen . . . Mark their spot on the first Monday . . . powder, paint and pictures . . . the usual aromatic litter of a dressing room. . . . Later I stood beside the stage manager in his corner. Act I of *Butterfly* was in full swing. And the Stage Manager? He was writing a letter home! Madame Butterfly's romance wasn't taking a hair out of him. . . . Light, colour, beauty, music. . . . 'See that Japanese lettering on those curtains?' says the director. 'That's real Japanese. It says: "Sadler's Wells Opera Company has the honour to present Madame Butterfly."'

No end to it!

I'm getting somewhat bewildered. Time I was away.

But the curtain comes down. The applause crescendoes into a mountain of enthusiasm. The chorus and principals, dresses swaying, head-dresses and make-up looking fantastically crude, sweep past me, on their way to the dressing room for a breather.

And behind comes the wardrobe lady, carrying Butterfly's wedding dress as if it were something truly precious.

Just a job? No, I don't quite think so.

Another angle of art.

The wardrobe mistress for the Sadler's Wells Opera Company working under the roof of the Grand Opera House in August 1945
IRELAND'S SATURDAY NIGHT

A very special element of this visit was the inclusion in the Sadler's Wells cast of the Belfast tenor James Johnston; here again Tyrone Guthrie had played a major role, in this case in the development of this great singer. During the Second World War there had been a shortage of tenors, and Guthrie had remembered the Belfast singer from his days with the BBC in Belfast. The story goes that he walked into the butcher's shop in Sandy Row where Johnston was working and offered him a job but that Johnston, associating Guthrie with the theatre, thought that he must have got the wrong man. In the end he was convinced, and agreed that Joan Cross, also from Sadler's Wells, could come to listen to him. He consented to join the company only on condition that if he didn't like it, he could come back to his old job in the butcher's shop.

Tenor James Johnston, who left his job as a butcher to become a principal singer with the Sadler's Wells Opera Company. His return visits after 1945 to the Grand Opera House were greeted with delight.
GRAND OPERA HOUSE

In his first season with the company he sang Jenik in *The Bartered Bride*, in opera houses in Düsseldorf and Berlin; his visit to the Grand Opera House, Belfast, stands out in many local memories. Leslie McCarrison ('Rathcol' of the *Belfast Telegraph*) recalls the excitement of his visit in *At Last, a Great Tenor*, by Leslie Gilmore.

Our delight knew no bounds when it was known that he would be heard as Jenik in that most delightful of operas, Smetana's *The Bartered Bride*, but there was a snag: the opera company management, presumably Joan Cross, refused to issue cast lists, and there was bitter disappointment when it was discovered that the local lad had been left out of all review performances but was appearing in the second cast. Local scribes got round the difficulty by bribing members of the ballet to locate 'Johnston nights' for us, and we remember the roar of laughter when the Marriage Broker (Owen Brannigan) asked Jenik, 'And who might you be?', and he was told in an unaltered Belfast accent, 'I'm a stranger in these parts.'

Johnston also delighted audiences as Pinkerton in *Madame Butterfly*. With the help of CEMA, the Sadler's Wells Opera Company (and James Johnston) returned to Belfast with *The Marriage of Figaro, Cavalleria rusticana* and *I Pagliacci* in July 1947.

The assistance, intervention and promotion of CEMA made a profound difference to the kind of entertainment that became available to audiences of the Grand Opera House. Now among the variety programmes was a range of new companies and artistes for the Belfast public to enjoy, all presented with the accompanying phrase 'in association with CEMA'. For the first time in many years ballet returned to the stage of the Grand Opera House. First came Ballet Joos, for a contemporary dance season, in 1946. The following year it was the turn of the mould-breaking Ballet Rambert in February and of the International Ballet Company, which came for two weeks in July and veered away from the popular repertoire to include *Everyman* by Richard Strauss, 'decorated' by Rex Whistler. In the same year CEMA helped to bring the Metropolitan Ballet, and in 1948 Sadler's Wells Ballet, directed by Ninette de Valois, and with Kenneth MacMillan in a minor role, visited Belfast. In 1949 there was enough confidence in public support to bring the International Ballet for three weeks, which included a gala night under the patronage of the Earl of Granville and the Honourable Basil Brooke.

CEMA also worked to bring high-quality drama to Northern Ireland. The Adelphi Guild Theatre brought plays like *It Depends What You Mean* by James Bridie, and *Hedda Gabler*, and it is something of a shock to realise that this was one of the very few Ibsen, or indeed European, plays that had been seen on the stage of the Grand Opera House until then. The Old Vic brought more traditional fare with *The Taming of the Shrew* and *The Alchemist*, which had Trevor Howard in the leading role and was a highlight of 1947. But without CEMA's help, Ilsley McCabe Productions, the Anew McMaster Company and the Firth Shephard All Stars Company all brought programmes that included such plays as *Edward, My Son*, *Life with Father* and *She Stoops to Conquer*.

It was around this time that the possibility of setting up an Ulster company of the Old Vic with a permanent, or semi-permanent, home in the Grand Opera House was seriously considered. The idea was that this company should tour, and tour ambitiously, not only to Glasgow, Liverpool and Bristol and to present a London season, but to Australia, New Zealand, Canada and the United States. According to Jack Loudan, head of CEMA at the time, 'With this in view, the search began for a building to house the Company in Belfast, a cinema or some other structure to be converted if a theatre itself were not available. At one time it seemed likely that the Grand Opera House could be acquired but that idea was reluctantly abandoned.' The impetus for the plan was halted by the fact that Tyrone Guthrie had decided to resign from theatre administration to concentrate on production; it was in this field that he was to play his next influential part in the development of the theatre in Northern Ireland.

Nineteen fifty-one was the year of the Festival of Britain. The festival marked the centenary of the Great Exhibition of 1851 and was intended to celebrate the 'astonishing progress of the United Kingdom in many fields – science and the arts, industry and agriculture, and the general well-being

For the Festival of Britain in 1951 Tyrone Guthrie brought together the best local talent in acting, writing and production; Guthrie is seated at the front on the right.
PUBLIC RECORD OFFICE OF NORTHERN IRELAND

of the people'. In a message to the people of Northern Ireland, its governor, the Earl of Granville, wrote as follows:

> That the Festival of Britain is being held in 1951, when the times are austere and the international outlook unsettling, is evidence of a resiliency of spirit that is characteristic of the British people. The Festival will be a source of new inspiration to all who value the British way of life and are ready to play their part in making the future bright and secure for the British Commonwealth as a whole.

Looking back now, the Festival of Britain accomplished much in the field of the arts, and from this perspective the activity and achievements of 1951 stand out today in sharp relief. There was a comprehensiveness about it, and a certainty of purpose, which gave it validity. The book *The Arts in Ulster* was conceived as a permanent record of Northern Ireland's contribution in poetry, drama, music and the visual arts. There were competitions with substantial prizes for a new play, a poem, a documentary film, for musical performance, for architecture, and for photography. An exhibition of Sir John Lavery's paintings was displayed in the Belfast Museum and Art Gallery (now the Ulster Museum), and the great mural by John Luke that is now such an integral part of Belfast's City Hall was commissioned. The BBC Irish Rhythms Orchestra and dancers under the direction of Patricia Mulholland worked together to give displays that included traditional and modern ballet. The Hallé Orchestra, under Sir John Barbirolli, came to Belfast.

Patricia Mulholland's Irish Ballet was one of the companies whose performances were presented in association with CEMA.
GRAND OPERA HOUSE

The Ulster Group Theatre and the Belfast Arts Theatre presented plays by St John Ervine, Lynn Doyle and George Farquhar, and as part of the contribution of the arts to the festival Tyrone Guthrie was asked to form and direct an Ulster Drama Company.

By this time Tyrone Guthrie already had a substantial reputation and had directed the greatest actors of the day. He once said that the director's duty was to 'make each rehearsal so amusing that the actors will look forward to the next one'. Laurence Olivier once stated that in 1944 Guthrie had given him 'the most priceless advice I've ever had from anybody'; this was when he was playing Sergius, an uninspiring part in Shaw's *Arms and the Man*. When Olivier complained about the tedious character, Guthrie had said, 'Well, of course, if you can't love Sergius, you'll never be any good in him, will you?' Olivier also said that Guthrie was 'shy of great human emotion'. When Olivier was playing with Jessica Tandy in *Henry V*, Guthrie had told him, 'You two go and do the love scene by yourselves, will you. I can't be bothered with that.'

Tyrone Guthrie agreed to form an Ulster Drama Company but only if new Ulster plays could be added to the existing repertoire. In an effort to find new work, or undiscovered old work, or work of other writers that could be adapted for the Northern Ireland stage, agents and researchers were asked to trawl their sources, and an Ulsterman, James Boyce, was sent to France. In the meantime, Guthrie had been working through the volumes of Ulster drama and had settled on George Shiels's *The Passing Day*, a play in which Jack Loudan felt that the dramatist observed the Ulster character with great clarity and which was 'full of sardonic humour and not without its share of bitterness'. For *The Passing Day*, Guthrie chose Tanya Moiseivitch as designer; she conceived a composite set on two levels, suiting the form of the play, which consisted of a reprise of the life of a prosperous country merchant.

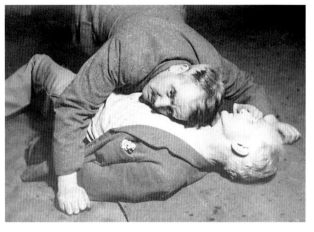

The writer of the second play designed his own set. John D. Stewart was a qualified engineer who had never written a play before but had gained a reputation as a writer for the radio. A London critic praised one of his contributions to the Home Service, saying, 'The power of radio to take the listener out of himself and show him the worlds behind the eyes of other men has never been used so skilfully.' CEMA felt that a young writer should be invited to contribute to Belfast's Festival of Britain programme and chose Stewart, who wrote *Danger, Men Working*, a serious comedy that examined the attitudes of Northern Ireland men to work. Jack Loudan summed up the theme. It was, he said, 'a play which poses, and tries to answer, one of the central public questions of the day: What makes men work?'

The Passing Day, a George Shiels play directed by Tyrone Guthrie for the Festival of Britain in 1951; Guthrie said the company gave a superb display of team work and in the leading role Joseph Tomelty scored a ringing success.
LINEN HALL LIBRARY

> Indeed, it goes deeper still and asks also the even more important private question: What is worth working for? The play presents a group of craftsmen and labourers engaged in building a new hospital in Northern Ireland at the present: it shows their response to various kinds of leadership. It shows at the same time the nobility and pathos of the industrial worker and the strength and weakness of those who direct his efforts. The author has handled this controversial material with goodwill to all, giving every man his say and condemning none.

The third choice for the festival was *The Sham Prince*, by Charles Shadwell, an eighteenth-century Irish comedy that had been rarely performed. *The Sham Prince* was rewritten and expanded by Jack Loudan, and sets were designed by a young Ulster architect, Henry Lynch Robinson. Loudan considered that the plot, which followed the hoaxing of a foppish young man, had a ring of reality about it. He quoted Shadwell's preface to the original play, which he believed may have reflected an actual happening.

GRAND OPERA HOUSE

> The play was written in five days, and by the actors got up in ten more. Everybody knows the occasion of it, and how well the town received it; therefore I hope the critics will be favourable to it; for I have made no alterations to it since its first acting; so that they may judge by the reading, the hurry I was in at the writing of it. As the design was to expose a public cheat, and to show the folly of some tradesmen, who were drawn in upon that occasion, I took care to do it so that even the people from whom I stole my characters could not take ill, and came to see themselves represented.

Set designs by Henry Lynch Robinson
for Tyrone Guthrie's production of
The Sham Prince in 1951
GRAND OPERA HOUSE

Tyrone Guthrie himself directed this interesting choice of three Irish dramas, and the casts included such familiar names as J.G. Devlin, Joseph Tomelty and James Young. They rehearsed in a room above a pub off Sandy Row, and the publican's name subsequently appeared in an honours list. Tyrone Guthrie was bemused by this 'ennoblement of our friend', presumably for services to the arts. At that stage he had not received any honours, but those who knew him said how proud he was of his later recognition, and especially of the doctorate conferred upon him by Queen's University, Belfast.

In addition to the drama, and as part of the Festival of Britain, the Grand Opera House hosted the International Ballet Company under Mona Inglesby in July, and in June another visit from the Royal Carl Rosa Opera Company, after an absence of fourteen years. By now a strong Northern Ireland connection with Carl Rosa had been formed. Rosa had set up his opera company in 1875 at the Princess's Theatre, London, with the intention of finding the best possible singers to sing opera in English, and paying particular attention to ensemble and production. After the First World War the Royal Carl Rosa Opera Company was the only remnant of a performing company left in Britain, but by 1918 a small touring company had been founded by Derryman H.B. Phillips, which merged soon after with the Carl Rosa company. In 1922 Phillips bought over Carl Rosa, and when Phillips died in 1949 his wife, Anette, also originally from Derry, took over the management. Anette Phillips had been a concert pianist in her own right, and was involved in all the artistic decisions, from casting to repertoire.

For the Festival of Britain programme Carl Rosa brought *Carmen* in its original version, *The Barber of Seville* in its complete form, Gounod's *Faust*, *Rigoletto*, *Il Trovatore*, *Cavalleria rusticana*, *I Pagliacci*, *Madame Butterfly* and *La Bohème*. The company was also asked to present the first performance of a new work by George Lloyd, called *John Solman*, which had been commissioned by the Arts Council of Great Britain. It was an exciting and challenging time for audiences of the Grand Opera House, but it was a time of change. In 1949 George Lodge, general manager of the Imperial Cinema and Cinematograph Theatres, had bought a controlling interest in the theatre.

GRAND OPERA HOUSE

Mona Inglesby, prima ballerina with the International Ballet Company, who visited the Grand Opera House in July 1951
LINEN HALL LIBRARY

6

PICTURE PALACE AND PAVAROTTI

GEORGE LODGE WAS, BY ALL ACCOUNTS, first and foremost a businessman. His business acumen led him to a place of pre-eminence amongst his peers, and he was a recipient of the OBE for his work. He seemed to have a good rapport with those with whom he worked and with his customers, and he had an ample capacity for embracing many different types of entertainment. He also seemed to have a generous and genuinely kind spirit. One story reported by the *Belfast Telegraph* tells of an incident in November 1951:

> When the staff of the Grand Opera House, Belfast went on duty this morning they could hardly believe their eyes – the theatre was full of people, all comfortably seated.
>
> *The occupants had not paid for their seats – they were there as guests of the management, and how it came about is related below.*
>
> Booking for the Christmas pantomime began this morning and at 9 o'clock on Wednesday evening a queue formed. At 11.0 there were 50 people there and as the night wore on the numbers increased.
>
> When Mr George Lodge O.B.E. managing director was on his way home he saw the queue and thought of the cold night.
>
> Mr Lodge opened the doors of the Opera House and the queue filed inside, took seats, and dozed or slept until the staff came on duty this morning to issue the tickets.
>
> No members of the staff were present during the night, but seats for latecomers were allocated by men who had joined the queue earlier. They made special arrangements for two children who arrived at 6.0 a.m.
>
> The first man in the queue got a pleasant surprise when booking opened. He was presented with complimentary tickets for a box on Christmas Night.

Lodge's Christmas goodwill extended as far as Crumlin Road jail. On at least two occasions he arranged for the pantomime artistes to entertain prisoners in the chapel of the prison. This was in addition to the monthly film shows that were arranged for the prisoners, although republican internees were not among the audience. The *Belfast Telegraph* noted an ironic twist when the pantomime *Old King Cole* was given in 1960: 'Before leaving for the prison comedian Harry Bailey received word from his wife that while she and two sons were watching television in their Malahide, Co. Dublin, home a burglar entered the kitchen and stole her purse, a £12 cheque and a bag of apples.'

Lodge's commitment to the success of the Grand Opera House was evident in his investment in that pantomime, *Old King Cole*, which was reported to have cost £27,000, whilst the 1958 production of *Cinderella*

Throughout the 1950s the pantomime tradition continued strongly; *Cinderella* was produced in 1952.
GRAND OPERA HOUSE

Opposite:
The Grand Opera House as cinema and Top Rank luxury theatre, *c.* 1960
BELFAST TELEGRAPH

The new Grand Opera House bar designed by Henry Lynch Robinson – stylish and modern in 1950, but the naked putti of the original design had to be removed for the sake of propriety.
MONUMENTS AND BUILDINGS RECORD

had amounted to an investment of only £10,000. There were two hundred costumes for the latest pantomime, some of them costing 'as much as £10'.

But Lodge had also a genuine love of the cinema. During the Festival of Britain he was one of the judges in the competition for a film documentary; he was described then as a keen amateur film producer. The success of the cinema in Belfast had started in 1910, when several picture palaces had opened, and the spread of picture houses, picture palaces and picture theatres continued steadily until 1929, when the arrival of the talkies prompted a second wave of development. In the thirties, the era of Clark Gable, familiar names like the Strand, the Astoria, the Curzon, the Ritz, the Windsor and the Regal opened; the new openings only came to a halt at the start of the Second World War. In the light of the glamorous attractions of the silver screen, the live variety productions at the Grand Opera House did well to survive.

But to Lodge's credit, despite his love of cinema he stayed true to the Grand Opera House as a theatre. In 1950 he instructed the architect Henry Lynch Robinson to make some improvements. The entrances to the stalls and the circle were combined – in 1950 there was no longer any need or wish to segregate the classes. The dress circle bar was remodelled fashionably and with style. A little of his style was considered too forward for 1950s Belfast, however: the naked putti who held the drapes at the bar were removed. By this time Lodge had begun to make experiments with cinema in the Grand Opera House but on a modest and sensitive level; they started in 1949 with a short film season featuring Laurence Olivier in *Hamlet*.

Michael Open has recorded the rise and fall of the cinemas of Belfast in *Fading Lights, Silver Screens*; he sees Lodge's position at this time as being very significant:

In Northern Ireland . . . the most important development of the Fifties was the sale of two major cinema circuits to the Rank Organisation in 1955. In that year, Rank built the Tivoli in Finaghy and bought two of the major cinema circuits in the province – the Curran circuit and Irish Theatres – making them (Rank) easily the largest and most influential film exhibitors in the Province. Starting under the direction of George Lodge, they dominated the film supply situation, ensuring that they always obtained the first choice of the most popular films.

The story of this takeover goes back to about 1953 when the Irish Theatres Group lost one of its founding fathers, Ferris (Paddy) Pounds. Into the power vacuum stepped George Lodge who had already, in his own right, and separate from Irish Theatres, control of the Imperial, Royal, Royal Hippodrome and Grand Opera House. Now, all the other directors of Irish Theatres were getting on in years and had no natural successors, so the attention of the company turned to the best way of dealing with possible takeovers.

Lodge was the natural person to deal with these negotiations and within two years, the deal with Rank had been completed. Moreover, Lodge realised that the deal could set up the eventual sale of the other cinemas over which he held sway.

In fact the Grand Opera House was poorly suited for showing films. The projection box was situated right above the back of the gallery, and the shape of the auditorium in comparison to the narrow screen was all wrong for most films, giving what is described as a 'keystone' effect. According to Michael Open, 'all in all, the use of the Grand Opera House as a cinema was no kind of success and even the most ardent cinephile is unlikely to regret that it has reverted to its original purpose'. The adaptation of the theatre made little sense, with a screen superimposed in the centre of the proscenium and patrons expected to watch films from the boxes, which were still in operation, at a very acute angle.

A 1950s programme cover
GRAND OPERA HOUSE

Despite the relentless march of the cinema, George Lodge still encouraged the Grand Opera House to be seen as the natural home for amateur dramatic and operatic companies, for the pantomime, and for the prestigious visiting companies. His attitude might be summed up in his approach to a poorly supported season by the Gate Theatre Company, which continued to visit the Grand Opera House on a regular basis. Micheál Mac Liammóir claimed a love-hate relationship with the city, writing on a visit he made in 1949 during the fraught period of the making of the film *Othello*, with Orson Welles:

> Impossible to fathom why I like this city, but I do. Admittedly a cold, ugly sort of place, even in this radiant northern April, its setting of windy mountains and dark shipyards, blotched with *fin-de-siècle* mansions and fussy streets full of plate glass and cake shops and trams, but there's something about it all, its fantastic predictability, its bleak bowler-hatted refusal of the inevitable – what is it? To arrive here from Rome within the space of two days is a fabulous experience; from that languorous immemorial embrace one passes to Brooke's 'rough male kiss of blankets'; Virgil and the Palatine Hill make way for the Bible and the bottle of Bushmills, and its air is that of a Business Man stepped right out of Alice's Wonderland and marching side by side with the Jabberwock through yards of bunting and gritty north-east winds to the rolling of drums.

Gate Theatre logo: Micheál Mac Liammóir and Hilton Edwards's Gate Theatre visited Belfast regularly, and it was the Grand Opera House which presented the first production of *Chimes at Midnight* in 1960, fulfilling a lasting ambition of Orson Welles to play Falstaff in this compilation of Shakespearean roles.
GATE THEATRE

The Gate made many very successful visits to the Grand Opera House, including a celebrated production of Maura Laverty's *Tolka Row*, with Micheál Mac Liammóir and Milo O'Shea in the cast. But the Belfast 'Business Man' of Mac Liammóir's fancy did not take to the repertoire offered by the Gate in 1955, which consisted of *A Slipper for the Moon*, *Not for Children* and *Henry IV*; the houses were so disappointing that emergency

The 'Veterans of Variety', who revived many memories of the music-hall in a 1950 tour. Included is Ella Shields (front row), the original 'Burlington Bertie'.
PUBLIC RECORD OFFICE OF NORTHERN IRELAND

In 1951 the popular touring production *Bless the Bride* enjoyed a three-week run at the Grand Opera House. Variety shows the same season included George Formby and Monte Rey, Radio's Romantic Singer.
LINEN HALL LIBRARY

measures had to be taken to put on the more popular *Liffey Lane* and *Tolka Row*, which themselves did not sell very well. George Lodge's reaction was to the point: he said that he had no objections 'to experiments in the presenting of plays, as long as John Citizen wants to go to see them'.

Throughout the 1950s, in addition to film showings, the theatre continued in its traditional role, and there were many highlights. Variety was still enjoyed, and in 1951 George Formby made a personal appearance at the end of a bill that included a dance team, a wizard, 'Scientific Nonsense' and a 'Sensational Hand Balancer'. Glamorous variety names succeeded each other – Ronnie Ronalde, the Voice of Variety, Monte Rey, Radio's Romantic Singer, Ivy Benson and her All Girls Band, Ted Ray, Semprini, the Melotones, Vera Lynn, the Beverley Sisters, Ronnie Hilton, Levante, the Greatest Name in Magic, the London Palladium's Les Compagnons de la Chanson, Frankie Howerd, Morecambe and Wise, Josef Locke, Joe Loss, Archie Andrews, Tommy Morgan, even Laurel and Hardy – and all the way through the fifties and into the sixties, the Grand Opera House kept alive its tradition of presenting the best of variety. A very successful show revived the best of the traditional music-hall. *Thanks for the Memory*, which boasted the original Burlington Bertie, Ella Shields, ran for two weeks, and raised a few sentimental tears. At the other extreme, in July 1950 the Grand Opera House experienced something quite novel (although it had occurred at least once before in the 1930s), when Tom Arnold's *Spectacular Ice Revue* was presented: the whole stage had become an ice-rink.

The Grand Opera House orchestra, now under Bob Marshall, was still playing and would have been required for all these shows as well as for a twice-nightly revue in 1953 from Jack Lewis, a skit on the Irving Berlin version, called *This Was the Army*, an all-male show that included items called 'The Awkward Squad' and 'The Girls Step Out'. A local revue made an appearance in the same year: *Easter Parade* starred James Young and was devised and produced by Young, from a book by Jack Loudan, Michael Bishop and Jack Hudson. Young became one of Belfast's best-loved comic actors, a master at capturing what was ridiculous in the life of the city, and consummate in portraying the quirks and foibles of its citizens. He had appeared on the stage of the Grand Opera House with the Savoy Players. Later he would go on to present his own brand of humour week after week, year after year, in the Group Theatre, which became synonymous with his name, and on television.

In its early days the Group Theatre appeared at the Grand Opera House in 1954 in *April in Assagh*, a light comedy by Joseph Tomelty. It had a cast that contained the best of Northern Ireland talent, with R.H. McCandless, Elizabeth Begley, Maurice O'Callaghan, Catherine Gibson, J.G. Devlin, Joseph Tomelty and James Ellis. In 1958, the Group presented *The Bonefire* in the Grand Opera House. A tragedy about 'the hatred between Protestants and Catholics in Ulster' by Gerard McLarnon, its sectarian theme attracted criticism from Belfast's lord mayor, who demanded, and won, changes in the script. *The Bonefire* had a similar cast to *April in Assagh*, but with the addition of the promising young actor Colin Blakely, and it was directed by Tyrone Guthrie. Within the decade, Blakely would return to the Grand Opera House in the distinguished company of the National Theatre. In the meantime, however, good and popular drama made its way to the stage of the Grand Opera House, although intermittently, through the fifties. Donald Wolfit brought a programme that included even Shakespeare plays, *Volpone* and *A New Way to Pay Old Debts*. A master of the dramatic, he was said to shake the curtains to encourage applause and continuing curtain calls.

The last of Britain's great actor–managers, Wolfit believed that everybody should have the opportunity to see Shakespeare's plays and translated this creed into practice through a series of provincial tours. He also had a reputation for self-aggrandisement, and was said to surround himself with inferior actors whom he made to hurry through their parts in order to make his own roles appear more impressive. He once omitted a whole scene from *Twelfth Night*, because he could not learn the lines, claiming that it must be the work of some other writer. 'I cannot learn it, and if I cannot learn it, Shakespeare did not write it!' One aspiring young actor, frustrated at the constant supply of poor parts in Wolfit's company, grew tired of asking for more challenging roles, and even more tired of coming on to announce, as the messenger in *Macbeth*, 'The Queen, my lord, is dead.' One evening, instead, he is said to have rushed on and stated, 'The Queen, my lord, is much better and is even now at dinner.'

The Old Vic's productions of *Macbeth* starred Rachael Roberts, Alan Dobie and Eric Porter; in *As You Like It*, Virginia McKenna played Rosalind. In 1953 a memorable staging of *Quadrille*, by Noël Coward, with the brilliant pairing of Alfred Lunt and Lynn Fontanne, and scenery and

It's Our Easter Parade – an early revue for the talents of James Young in 1953
GRAND OPERA HOUSE

costumes by Rex Whistler, came direct from the Phoenix Theatre, and was a notable coup for the Grand Opera House. The Lunts at this stage of their career were the talk of the theatre world and posed as a very fashionable couple. They said of themselves, 'We can be bought, but we can't be bored', while Noël Coward wrote in his diary in the year in which they visited Belfast, 'They are deeply concerned with only three things – themselves, the theatre (in so far as it concerns themselves) and food – good, hot food.' Whether they were fed or bored in Belfast is not recorded, but the management must have been content. A popular couplet asserted:

> If you want a play to run many a munt
> Get Lynn Fontanne and Alfred Lunt.

London Festival Ballet programme
LINEN HALL LIBRARY

Opera and ballet continued to visit Belfast. Finally, the story of the Royal Carl Rosa Opera Company came to a close, but not before Kenneth McKellar had appeared in its casts in 1953. Kenneth Montgomery, later to be artistic director of Opera Northern Ireland, went to see the Carl Rosa company perform *Tannhäuser* in the 1950s, at the age of about twelve. Sitting high in the gods at a Saturday matinée, he was bitterly disappointed by his first experience of opera and left at the interval. Ten years later, he was taught at the Royal College of Music by the principal soprano in that production of *Tannhäuser*. 'That was the worst thing we ever did – you were quite right to leave,' she said. The Carl Rosa company was succeeded at the Grand Opera House by tours from D'Oyly Carte and Covent Garden; the London Festival Ballet under Anton Dolin also came regularly throughout the fifties.

The management of the theatre sold its productions vigorously. Advertisements in the local press were bright and novel. In an effort to bring in an audience from outside Belfast, patrons were invited to make up a 'party from your town', and special terms were offered for 'first houses for Provincial Parties'.

The shift from fifties into sixties marked a change. Belfast suddenly seemed a more prosperous and a slightly more sophisticated city. Motorways were planned, boutiques began to emerge, pop concerts took place culminating in the overwhelming excitement of the Beatles and the Rolling Stones at the Ritz and the Beatles again, at the King's Hall, and the television set dominated most sitting rooms. American culture was beginning to take a gradual hold on the United Kingdom, and the idea was put about in October 1960 that the Grand Opera House might be sold for use as a bowling alley. While firmly scotching the rumour, George Lodge left the door open. The *Belfast Telegraph*'s property correspondent reported that when asked if there was any possibility of the Grand Opera House being sold in the foreseeable future, Lodge replied, 'It is always for sale, as is all my property, including the suit I am wearing, if I get the right price.'

The *Belfast Telegraph* correspondent went on to report that in Britain the new bowling alleys had proved profit-making ventures only in very big areas with large teenage populations, and that until they had proved more popular in the provincial centres of Britain, Belfast was unlikely to have a bowling alley.

In any case the Grand Opera House was dismissed as a possibility for bowling because of its sloping floor. But George Lodge's assertion that anything he had was for sale was duly justified, and in 1960 Rank Odeon became the owner of the Grand Opera House, though not before George Lodge had played a final important part in one of the most bizarre episodes in the history of Irish theatre.

The friendship of Hilton Edwards and Micheál Mac Liammóir with Orson Welles had been fruitful and turbulent since Welles had arrived unannounced, brash and charismatic at the door of the Gate in 1931. After frustrations and rows, triumphs and disasters, in the late 1950s Welles suddenly decided that he would like to fulfil a long-held ambition, to act the role of Falstaff in a compilation of extracts from Shakespeare's plays. Edwards and Mac Liammóir agreed to help with the project, which was conceived as *Chimes at Midnight*, and when Lodge heard about the idea, he offered the Grand Opera House for a week, providing Welles was in the cast. As the planning progressed, problems multiplied. They came to a head when Welles and Mac Liammóir failed to agree on which role Mac Liammóir should play, a disagreement that resulted in Mac Liammóir's withdrawal. In rehearsals Welles caused havoc by the vagaries of his behaviour. Christopher Fitz-Simon takes up the story:

> The company moved to Belfast on Sunday, 21 February 1960, for an opening on Tuesday 24 [*sic*]. The whole of Monday morning and afternoon was taken up with technical rehearsal, and the dress rehearsal lasted for twelve hours, with Welles on the stage constantly suggesting brilliant changes to Edwards, who was shouting and spluttering from the stalls. Mac Liammóir arrived from Dublin and crept into a dark corner of the dress circle, occasionally emerging to whisper comments into Edwards' ear. He refused to speak to Welles, and remained in the background, dressed in black, throughout the run of the play.
>
> On the opening night, Orson Welles was not sure of his lines, but the company rose to him and helped him out, in the way that even the most misused actors invariably do at times, and he created a forceful impression through the sheer power of personality.

The actor who took over the role of Hal was Keith Baxter. Eddie McIlwaine, a journalist at the *Belfast Telegraph* who covered many Grand Opera House stories and who has enormous affection and respect for the theatre, discovered a link and a fresh view of this extraordinary episode when Keith Baxter returned to play in *Dangerous Corner* in Belfast in 1995.

> Distinguished actor Keith Baxter, 61, admits he will have a tear in his eye when he steps on stage at the Opera House next Monday for the first time in 35 years.
>
> For it was at the theatre in Belfast in 1960 that legendary Orson Welles singled him out for stardom.

Micheál Mac Liammóir in
Darkness at Noon
GATE THEATRE

'He changed the course of my life forever that February night at the Opera House,' said Baxter.

He has waited all these years to return to the theatre which has a special place in his heart. . . . But early in 1960, he was washing dishes in a London restaurant when he auditioned successfully for the role of Prince Hal in Chimes at Midnight, a Shakespeare adaptation starring Welles and directed by him too.

'We were opening in Belfast and the dress rehearsal had been a disaster. Another young actor lied to me that Welles who was Falstaff didn't like me as Hal after all. I was going to bed in my digs at Lisburn Road, depressed and thinking I was a failure, when I was summoned by Welles to the Grand Central Hotel for a champagne supper. He told me what a wonderful talent I had and that one day I would be the toast of Broadway.'

But six weeks later Chimes at Midnight ended its short tour in Dublin and Baxter was on the ferry going home.

'I had no prospects and at 26, I was going back to dish washing. Suddenly on the deck I smelt cigar smoke and Orson appeared beside me. He told me he was going to make a film of Chimes at Midnight and that I would be in it. He kept his promise and the movie with John Gielgud, Jeanne Moreau and myself is reckoned to be one of the best he ever directed.

'I did go on to star on Broadway and have a wonderful life. I owe it all to him and it is a delight to return to the theatre where it began.'

The reviews of the Belfast production of *Chimes at Midnight* were mixed, and it moved to the Gaiety Theatre in Dublin and then petered out, but it was a dramatic curtain for the era of George Lodge.

The new owner, Rank Odeon, now made what it said was improvements to the theatre; these included new carpets, new tip-up seats (which were smaller and more tightly aligned with reduced leg room), better ventilation, and up-to-date projection equipment. The company also carried out some redecoration, which it claimed was in the style of the building, and it claimed to have improved the entrance. In fact, it turned the pit bar on Great Victoria Street into the main entrance hall with plate glass doors, corridors and crude new staircases.

Hand in hand with the renovations to the theatre, Rank Odeon was carrying out changes to the Hippodrome theatre next door, and while that was going on thirty films were shown at the Grand Opera House, beginning with Walt Disney's *Swiss Family Robinson* and *The Big Fisherman*. Subsequently, however, the Rank Organisation preferred to show classic films in the Grand Opera House, favouring such films as *A Man for All Seasons* and *The Taming of the Shrew*. The new owners promised a mixture of films and live shows:

Future live-show presentations will include the New Lyric Opera Company's production of the 'Desert Song' on October 2 and the Ulster Operatic Society's 'Kismet' on October 30.

From then onwards this policy of a mixture of live shows and films will continue and negotiations are in hand for ballet and opera productions in early 1962. It is also hoped to make arrangements for a pantomime over the

Costume design by Mercy Hunter for Patricia Mulholland's production of *The Dream of Angus Og*, 1963.
GRAND OPERA HOUSE

Christmas period.

The Rank Organisation ran its empire from offices above the Capital Cinema on the Antrim Road, where Roy Eveleigh directed its affairs. A small man, but liable to be big in commanding orders, his desk sat on a raised platform on one side of the office so that those employees who were summoned to his presence had to look up to him, literally.

However, there was a less than sure touch later in 1961 from the new owners concerning the vital question of a pantomime. 'Chichester' of the *Belfast Telegraph* was worried: 'With Christmas less than eight weeks away, I learned today that a big question mark hangs over Belfast's traditional pantomime, highlight of the festive season for thousands.' No one in the Grand Opera House could help 'Chichester' with his enquiries, and when he contacted the top brass in London, he got no further: 'Staging a pantomime in the Opera House is entirely a matter for our chaps in Belfast. It has nothing to do with London.' The *Belfast Telegraph* columnist voiced the anxieties of many.

> Christmas without a pantomime would be a big disappointment. It's almost as much a part of the Yuletide season as turkey and plum pudding. And I find it especially hard to imagine the Opera House without it. For pantomime has always held a place of special affection in the theatre.

The year 1961 was a significant one in Ulster's theatre in other ways. The Empire Theatre in Victoria Square, another building that held a very special place in the affections of the people of Belfast, through its history of variety, drama and even circus, was demolished for redevelopment. On the brighter side, the Arts Theatre opened new premises in Botanic Avenue, and in 1962 the new Arts Council for Northern Ireland, suc-

Luciano Pavarotti made his British debut as Lieutenant Pinkerton in *Madame Butterfly* at the Grand Opera House in 1963; he is seen here with local singer Margaret Smyth, who sang Kate Pinkerton.
MARGARET SMYTH

ceeding CEMA, organised a Little Festival, to mark the 350th anniversary of the granting of a charter to the City of Belfast. The festival included Irish ballet from Patricia Mulholland's company, productions from the Abbey Theatre, the first visit from the London Ballet Company and productions from the Grand Opera Society of Northern Ireland.

The Grand Opera Society of Northern Ireland had been founded by John Lewis-Crosby and John Patterson to fill the void caused by the demise of the Carl Rosa company. The annual productions were mounted in conjunction with an Italian impresario, who would bring to Belfast complete productions, conductors and a series of promising young singers, most of them Italian. Anna Moffo sang Gilda for the society, and in the *Madame Butterfly* of 1963 was a young tenor who was on his way up. His name was Luciano Pavarotti, and it was at the Grand Opera House that he made his British debut. Margaret

Dawson Allen.
Kenneth Anderson.
Desmond Andrews
Laurence Andrews.
Ronnie Andrews.
Richard Bell.
Robert Bell.
Desmond Bingham.
Clifford Boyd.
William Boyles.
Kenneth Brackenridge.
Ronnie Brackenridge.
Philip Breakey.
William Breakey.
Bruce Carswell.
Lawrence Chambers.
Ronald Chambers
William Chambers.
Edward Conway.

Maurice Corbett.
Trevor Crothers.
John Davidson.
Ivor Donaldson.
Eric Duncan.
Brian Ellis.
Maynard English.
Mervyn Farrell.
Eric Ferguson.
William Finlay.
James Fitzgerald.
Joe Flaherty.
Ronald Flude.
Desmond Gettinby.
Jack Giffin.
Walter Giffin.
Donald Gilbert.
Alan Gilbert.
Stanley Gilbert.

David Gilfillan.
Clifford Gilmer.
Allen Glennie.
Harry Gordon.
Norman Graham.
Sam Graham.
Frank Haddow.
David Hall.
Eugene Hamilton.
Trevor Hamilton.
Ronnie Harbinson.
Graham Harron.
Robin Harte.
Lyle Hatrick.
Lindsay Hawe.
Harris Healey.
George Hegan.
William Hegan.
Ronald Henry.

John Hewitt.
George Holland.
Garnet Holt.
Desmond Hunt.
Alan Huss.
Brian Inskip.
Sam Irwin.
Raymond Jack.
Kenneth Johnston.
Herbert Lavery.
John Ledlie.
Maurice Logue.
Michael Longley.
Peter Longley.
William Lowry.
Ronald Macartney.
Brian Mackintosh.
David Mahood.
David Mills,

William Miskimmin.
Ross Moffett.
David Moncrieff.
William Moreland.
Ian Morrow.
Robert Morrow.
Campbell Murray.
Crossley Musson.
Alan McAlinden.
Terry McBurney.
George McCartney.
Gordon P. McCaw.
Douglas McClure.
Reggie McClure.
William McConkey.
Thomas McCormick.
Thomas McCrea.
Harry McCullough.

David McDowell.
Derek McKeague.
Allan McKee.
Andrew McKee.
Norman McKenna.
Bobby M'Killop.
Richard M'Kinney.
John M'Knight.
Derek McMahon.
Thomas McMullan.
James McQuillan.
Roy McTaggart.
Eric McWilliams.
Derek Neill.
James Neill.
Patrick Ormonde.
Reggie Patterson.
Samuel Prenter.

The cast of the Gang Show, 1953; several members went on to make significant contributions to the cultural and commercial life of Northern Ireland.

MARGARET WARING

Smyth, from Belfast, sang Kate Pinkerton to his Lieutenant Pinkerton, and has nothing but fond memories of the large and amiable young singer. She remembers her singing teacher, Minna Patterson, who taught with her husband John, remarking, 'Enjoy him while you can – that voice is going to the top.'

Some time later, Margaret Smyth and a friend went to see him sing at Covent Garden. As they waited at the stage door, having been stopped by the door-keeper, impassive and unpassable like the keepers of all stage doors, Pavarotti swept out. Catching sight of her, he brushed aside the Covent Garden fraternity, cried with great good humour 'Ah Belfast!' and treated her to a Pavarotti embrace of spontaneous and genuine pleasure. Those who have met him in recent years say that he claims to remember his Belfast appearance well, because it came at such an important time in his career.

In 1963, the Grand Opera House did well for opera. Sadler's Wells presented five operas, giving Belfast its first chance to see and hear Benjamin Britten's opera *Peter Grimes*. (Such is the conservative taste of

de Rainey.
rdon Redpath.
. Reid.
old Robb.
an Roberts.
vor Shannon.
tie Simpson.
nneth Smart.
rry Smith.
bert Smith.
nley Smith.
nis Smyth.
n Snowdon.
bert Spence.
hur Stewart.
vid Stewart.
uel Stewart.
es Taylor.

Maurice Taylor.
Austin Thompson.
Norman Thompson.
Jim Toland.
Norman Trimble.
Ronald Trimble.
James Turner.
Thorpe Walker.
Ronald Wallace.
Howard Williams.
Russell Williams.
Robert Wilson.
Phillip Witherspoon.
James Woodburne.
Gordon Woods.
William Yarr.
Joe Young.

Belfast audiences that very few opera managers have risked a Britten opera here.) In the same year D'Oyly Carte's popular repertoire attracted record audiences to the Grand Opera House.

The world of amateur opera continued to use the Grand Opera House through the 1950s and 1960s, and so did the Ulster Drama Festival, but a new and totally different group of young amateurs took to the boards in this period with the first of a series of Gang Shows. The first Belfast Gang Show was staged in the Opera House in 1951, and it followed in the tradition of the Scout Gang Shows that had been begun by Ralph Reader in 1932 at the Scala Theatre, London, and had gone from strength to strength. Ralph Reader, who remained the inspiration behind these shows and often became involved with writing and producing Gang Shows outside London, came to Belfast rehearsals in 1951, 1953, 1955 and 1958. In 1953 he wrote a song specially for that year's show. The first Gang Show was reported in the *Northern Whig* on 16 April 1951:

Not since Irving Berlin brought 'This is the Army' to Ulster has the Belfast Opera House stage risked bursting its seams to accommodate so big, so zesty, so tuneful, so colourful and so thoroughly all round entertaining a production as 'The Gang Show' which the Boy Scouts of Belfast presented there on Saturday afternoon. . . . It is, and has, everything, music (a dozen extremely catchy songs), dancing (all male ballet and fairy sequences devised and produced by Leila Corry), humour, recitations, solos and a number of ingeniously conceived burlesque sketches.

Gang Show programme cover, 1967
GRAND OPERA HOUSE

The first Gang Show was put on for two Saturday matinées, but by 1953 the show was running for a week. The 1953 programme expresses the indebtedness of the Belfast County Scout Council to 'George Lodge OBE, JP, and the management of the Grand Opera House for their encouragement of this venture', and also goes out of its way to thank the backstage crew: 'A very special "Thank You" is due to Mr A.D. Hopla, the Theatre Stage Manager, and his staff for their most valuable and willing help given at all times.' John Jordan, who was later to become technical manager of the theatre, worked with Hopla at the start of his career, and confirms that the programme note was sincere. Hopla was a very nice man.

The enthusiasm, team spirit, and love of boisterous fun that many can remember as an integral part of growing up in the fifties are reflected in the same programme:

Every member of the Gang is an active Boy Scout or Rover Scout and every

GRAND OPERA HOUSE

member of the Cast is prepared to take his place in the chorus. If a chap is lucky enough to sing a verse or act in a sketch he is just as likely to be in the chorus in the next item. All performers are active Scouts and no 'stars' are strict conditions of membership. The Gang like to feel that they are very much a team.

Ralph Reader recalled the atmosphere of the Belfast rehearsals in his book *This Is the Gang Show*:

Boys are mostly the same the world over, but if an extra bit of warmth can come from any one set then I would award the palm to the Ulster Lads. I don't know why, but even the smallest bloke made me feel I had known him for years. They had a passion for work, and I worked them good and hard. They were on the floor every second I was with them and they loved it. . . .

Ralph Reader with some members of the 1961 Gang Show at the Grand Opera House; although he attended rehearsals intermittently from 1951 to 1958, 1961 was the only time he was in the audience for an actual performance.
MARGARET WARING

Billy's sister Mabel plays the piano for all the rehearsals, and there is, to my way of thinking, a great deal to be said for the presence of a lady during these hectic periods. Somehow they cast a sort of 'niceness' over the hectic prancing and rushing around, and they remain cool in the most hectic moments.

'Billy' was the Boy Scouts' Commissioner for Ulster, Judge William Johnston, and he was succeeded as producer jointly by R.J. Brown, R.J.C. Boyd, and W. Chambers, who carried on the tradition of the Gang Shows at intervals at the Grand Opera House until they moved to the Harberton Theatre in 1975.

While the Gang Shows represented some of the talents of one section of Belfast's population, productions on the stages of Belfast's theatres in the 1960s rarely addressed the vital issues facing Northern Ireland. In fact, in one of the most divisive and controversial episodes in the history of drama in Northern Ireland took place in 1960, when the Group Theatre accepted a new play by Sam Thompson, a Belfast shipyard worker, called *Over the Bridge*. Thompson's play handled the problem of sectarianism in the Belfast shipyard, and the theatre directors themselves later took fright at the uncompromising nature of the script and demanded cuts, refusing to mount a production and effectively ending the role of the Group as a serious theatre. They were resolved 'not to mount any play which would offend or affront the religious or political beliefs or sensibilities of the man in the street'. In the end, after a determined search for a theatre by Sam Thompson and the actor James Ellis, assisted by politician, trade unionist and writer Paddy Devlin, it was the Dublin-owned Empire that took the risk, and the play ran to packed houses for three weeks, to intelligent enthusiasm.

Hilton Edwards had met Sam Thompson when he came up from Dublin to the Grand Opera House to light *The Importance of Being Oscar*. This, like *I Must Be Talking to My Friends*, was a very successful one-man show by Micheál Mac Liammóir; both were toured internationally. He confesses to having been nervous of meeting the writer, conscious that his own very English accent and manner might have been off-putting, but he found Thompson 'warm, generous, co-operative, exceedingly friendly' and with a conviction that the theatre 'was the only place you can get democracy, where people can object'. Paddy Devlin described Sam Thompson as someone he liked instantly:

> He was an uncomplicated straight-shooter who always seemed to be smouldering on the verge of explosion into flames at the sight or sound of injustice or deceit. Everybody within earshot knew where Sam stood on any issue. If they did not it never took Sam long to tell them.

Thompson had hoped that the same company that had mounted *Over the Bridge* would be able to produce his new play *The Evangelist*, a powerful drama which dealt with the hypocrisy of religious fundamentalism, but it proved too expensive for them to stage, and Hilton Edwards agreed to take it on.

In 1963 Sam Thompson's *The Evangelist*, produced with Ray McAnally in the lead, and with a strong cast which included T.P. McKenna, was premièred at the Grand Opera House before moving to the Gaiety Theatre, Dublin. Although reservations were expressed about the quality of the work as a whole, it was agreed that it was an important piece of drama, and the transfer to Dublin of a good play about Belfast was seen as equally significant.

In 1965 *Stephen D*, by the Dublin Festival Company, played at the Grand Opera House to packed and appreciative audiences. But there was no doubt about the highlight of 1966. In November, the National Theatre with Sir Laurence Olivier, Frank Finlay and Colin Blakely came with memorable productions of *Love for Love* and *Hobson's Choice*. It was a notable and much-appreciated visit, and Bangor's favourite son was received with just pride. The custom was to hold a midday press conference, and when Betty Lowry attended it as drama critic of the *Belfast Telegraph* she asked Sir Laurence the natural question – what did he think of Colin Blakely. 'Oh, splendid,' was the airy reply. Like John Gilpin and Belinda Wright in the London Festival Ballet, the National Theatre's visit was a contribution to Festival '66. The idea of a festival in Belfast was indicative of new and positive thinking in the arts in Ulster. But the shape of Belfast itself was changing, important economic tides were running, political events were moving fast and, before long, there would be sinister figures in the shadows.

The Evangelist, written by Sam Thompson (top) and starring Ray McAnally. The 1963 production was directed by Hilton Edwards.
GRAND OPERA HOUSE

7

'FLAK JACKETS
AND EVENING DRESS . . .'

THE IDEA OF A 'NATIONAL' THEATRE for Northern Ireland had been under active consideration since the post-war activity engineered by Tyrone Guthrie. Indeed during the Second World War, to everyone's surprise, six hundred people had turned up to a meeting in the Belfast College of Technology on a rainy Saturday night to hear Micheál Mac Liammóir talking about the need for an Arts Theatre in Ulster. In the 1950s there had been support for a plan for a Civic Theatre (which included the backing of the Minister of Home Affairs, Bill Craig), and an Ulster Theatre Council was set up under the chairmanship of Sir Tyrone Guthrie, who was now also Chancellor of Queen's University. The definition of the term 'national' in the context of the theatre had never been properly identified, and when the question of partition became a factor, the project foundered. Most of the support simply vanished after Guthrie made a controversial speech in October 1964 in Belfast's City Hall, in which he referred to the border in the context of a theatre council:

> It is up to us to abolish this border. It may not be in our lifetime that the political border is abolished, but let us in our lifetime see that it is abolished in the minds of those of us who have enjoyed the advantages of university education by joining one another in goodwill and understanding of the other fellow's point of view, political or commercial.

If the question of a national or civic theatre had gone into abeyance, there was still active concern about housing the arts, particularly drama, in Belfast. The Grand Opera House was not seen as an effective possibility because of its ownership and present use. The Arts Council Annual Report of 1963–64 examined the problem of facilities:

> Visiting companies play in the main at the Grand Opera House and the King George VI Youth Centre. The latter is not designed as a theatre. By arrangement with Odeon (NI) the former is used as a Rank Organisation cinema. It is therefore a matter of great importance that the representations of various bodies for the creation of a theatre complex in Belfast should not go unheeded. . . . Anyone who has misgivings about the wisdom or desirability of such a project should consider the liberal provision of theatre complexes in towns throughout Germany which have a quarter of the population of Belfast. This is an issue on which we cannot afford to procrastinate. . . . The Arts Council cannot build theatres. It is up to those progressive communities wishing to provide these civilised amenities, and to attract new industries, to consider how best this need can be met either by erecting new buildings, or modifying existing ones under expert guidance which can be obtained through this Council.

Opposite:
Stairway leading to the Grand Opera House boxes before restoration work began in 1976
MONUMENTS AND BUILDINGS RECORD

In the mid-1960s the Arts Council of
Northern Ireland was responsible for
the conversion of the Troxy Cinema
on the Shore Road into the Grove
Theatre. It held an audience of one
thousand but was never considered an
ideal venue for theatre.
ULSTER FOLK AND TRANSPORT MUSEUM

Shortly afterwards, however, despite having earlier disclaimed responsibility
for the provision of theatre facilities, the Arts Council was responsible for
facilitating the conversion of the Troxy Cinema on the Shore Road into
the Grove Theatre, which was capable of holding an audience of over one
thousand and hosted visiting companies in the next few years. When the
Lyric Theatre took its productions there in 1965–66 from its fifty-seater
theatre in Derryvolgie Avenue, it multiplied its audience to three hundred,
although three hundred spectators in the Grove was an uncomfortably
sparse audience, and the Arts Council soon acknowledged that in spite of
improved acoustics and amenities, and the valued enterprise and generous
co-operation of the Grove's owners, 'it is not really suitable for initiating a
continuous and progressive artistic policy'. Although the Grove may not
have been the theatre aficionado's idea of heaven, it did play an important
part in the history of drama in Northern Ireland. It was here that Kenneth
Branagh had his first introduction to the stage. He describes it in his autobiography *Beginning*:

> I had my first trip to the theatre: a production of *A Christmas Carol* at the
> Grove Theatre, which starred Joseph Tomelty, with whose daughter, Frances,
> I would later work. I was enthralled by the tale itself – which promoted a
> great love for Dickens – but also by the nature of the performance. They were
> there, actually in front of me, *being*. There was no other word for it. Magic.

In 1965 the Arts Council stated that 'there were only the mettlesome
popular managements at the Arts and the Group and the twelve annual
weeks of live theatre at the Grand Opera House' to serve the cause of

theatre in the city. It began to feel its way to overcome both the frustration of the lack of an indigenous theatre with a consistent artistic policy, and the necessity of engaging professional drama companies *ad hoc* either locally or from Britain. And it was still acutely aware of the lack of a decent building for theatre.

Musically, similar problems had been resolved with the establishment of the Ulster Orchestra, which had a coherent agenda, and a natural home in the Ulster Hall. Several promising schemes for theatre were considered and aborted. One of the most likely proposals centred around the Plaza in Chichester Street, a well-known 'ballroom of romance', the most renowned meeting place in 1950s Belfast, and butt of many jokes. The Plaza's success was at its height in the 1950s when the showbands toured Ireland to great popularity, but the discos of the 1960s were overtaking the dance halls, and the Arts Council and the owner of the Plaza, Mecca Ltd, advanced quite far in discussions, with the aim of creating from the building a well-equipped theatre with facilities on a par with those offered by Birmingham, Glasgow or Nottingham.

Within a year this plan fell through; Mecca withdrew its scheme 'in face of the stern economic situation'. In retrospect, it was perhaps fortunate for the future of the Grand Opera House that this ambitious and costly project did not absorb Arts Council aspirations and funding. But as this scheme foundered, a new and vital chapter opened up as, in 1968, the Lyric Theatre moved from its old home in Derryvolgie Avenue to a new theatre in Ridgeway Street. The struggle to get this new theatre built had not been easy, but in the end the Arts Council had supported the venture, and the Lyric's contribution to drama in Belfast increased in significance, as it went on to provide a continuous repertory programme of important productions and offered a platform for new writers.

In the Arts Council Report for 1967–68 the idea that there should be a place of common ground for 'highbrow and lowbrow audiences alike' was strongly expressed. The Grove Theatre was the only building that supplied this need; the Arts Council was still contracted to the Grove to fill the theatre for a minimum period each year, and the report states, with perhaps a touch of desperation, 'here a determined effort must be made to establish a continuing policy over a period, even if it means opening a season on a limited budget and going on only so long as public support makes it possible'.

In 1969, in keeping with the policy of using the Grove, Sir Tyrone Guthrie directed *Macook's Corner* there. In the same year, in the Ulster drama finals, still clinging to the Grand Opera House, the Ilford Players had the nerve to produce the same play, even though Guthrie was the adjudicator. But the amateur finals week was one of the very few live events to take place at the Grand Opera House that year. There was no opera season in 1969 as the Northern Ireland Opera Trust was just coming into existence.

In 1969, the Troubles hit Belfast with their full and bloody force. In August, two doors down from the stage door in Glengall Street, families

Shankill Road, Belfast, August 1968:
steel-helmeted policemen are seen at a
burning barricade, surrounded by the
debris of several days' rioting
BELFAST TELEGRAPH

who had escaped the worst civic strife and social upheaval of our times in
Ireland took refuge from their burning homes in the rooms of the Belfast
Central Mission at the back of the Grosvenor Hall, while from the station
in Great Victoria Street, beside the theatre, other families from other parts
of the city escaping a similar plight fled to Dublin for refuge.

There is no doubt that in the violence and turmoil that followed, normal life in Belfast was altered. There was certainly very little night life.
Throughout much of the seventies, the centre of Belfast was eerily quiet at
night. Few pubs remained open and few buses ran after nine o'clock.
Belfast people chose to take their amusement in neighbourhoods where
they felt safe, or in their own homes. A weekend escape to Dublin, or
London, became extremely popular. The Arts Theatre closed in 1971 but
the Lyric remained open, and in spite of the problems of operating in a city
where bombs aimed at destroying its commercial centre had become common, the pantomime *Aladdin* was put on at the Grand Opera House in
1971, with Frances Tomelty in the lead role, and the Northern Ireland
Opera Trust gallantly presented *Carmen* and *Tosca* in the same year.

Indeed the Northern Ireland Opera Trust, under its administrator,

Alison Taggart, deserves great credit for keeping going through the worst years. The opera critic for the *Financial Times* and *Opera* magazine, Elizabeth Forbes, recalls the difficulties and quirks of operating in Belfast at this time, writing in an Opera Northern Ireland programme in 1988:

I first came to Belfast in 1976. Flying from Heathrow to Aldergrove, I was met by the Administrator of Northern Ireland Opera Trust. In those days the airport was hermetically sealed and visitors had to wait in a special hut, in limbo. The Administrator had been waiting there a couple of hours. Belfast, she assured me as we drove into the city by the scenic route, was absolutely quiet. On reaching the top of the hill, from which the best views could be obtained, I realised that her information was a little out of date. The smoke from seven or eight fires rose up towards us. It soon became apparent that one of these fires had destroyed the hotel where I intended to stay. In front of a forlorn pile of smoking ruins, the Artistic Director of Northern Ireland Opera Trust stood waiting, to direct us to another hotel outside the city. That evening *La Bohème* was given with great success in the ABC Cinema. The sets, on loan from Glyndebourne Touring Opera (or those of them that could fit on the shallow stage of the ABC) were much admired. After the performance, there was, as so often in Belfast, a party. It was only after returning to my hotel that I realised my family and friends, who had seen the smoking ruins of the hotel in Belfast on television, thought I might be under those ruins.

The dramatic events of my first visit to Belfast continued the next day. The opera that evening was Donizetti's *Lucia di Lammermoor*, staged by an Austrian producer making his local – and British – debut. During the morning a car, believed to contain a bomb, was parked outside the ABC and the whole area was cordoned off. I spent the next few hours, together with the Artistic Director, sitting in a coffee bar trying to calm the producer, who showed signs of hysteria as the day wore on. It was not till about an hour before curtain-up that the bomb was defused – or found to be non-existent, I never discovered which – and we could get into the ABC. The scenery for *Lucia* was mainly black curtains, but the performance, with an unflappable American Lucia, was excellent.

The following spring I returned to Belfast. This year the operas were *Rigoletto* and *Faust*. As there was currently no suitable hotel available, the singers (and the London press) stayed in the Queen's University Senior Common Room. The singers took it in turns to do the cooking and the tenor from *Faust*, who came from the South of France, made a delicious paella for lunch one day. There were about a dozen of us round the table, but the tenor had made sufficient for about forty, so the Senior Common Room was eating paella for days on end.

That year, although no actual incidents occurred, there were several false alarms. One performance of *Rigoletto* was interrupted three times while the cinema had to be cleared. It was raining and I sat in the back of a car with the soprano (Marguerite), who so far had only sung one line, and the baritone (Valentine), who had his extended death scene still to come and was worried in case he should catch cold.

The determination of the Northern Ireland Opera Trust board and

By 1971 the Troubles had hit Belfast hard, but a pantomime was produced at the Grand Opera House with Frances Tomelty as Aladdin.
GRAND OPERA HOUSE

The Grand Opera House before restoration, considered by the Arts Council of Northern Ireland 'so scathed' that no touring companies could visit
MONUMENTS AND BUILDINGS RECORD

management to keep on operating was typical of the attitude in Belfast throughout the twenty-five years from 1969 to 1994. In 1978 the ABC Cinema was burnt down, and the Northern Ireland Opera Trust, not to be defeated, gave some concert performances of *La Traviata* in the Common Hall of the Royal Belfast Academical Institution, down the road, but of all the arts organisations that needed a fitting space in which to work, it was the providers of opera who suffered most from the lack of the Grand Opera House as a working theatre.

This state of affairs had begun in 1972 when, with the situation in Belfast very dark, Rank Odeon closed the Grand Opera House and sold the site to property developers. This was the time when millions of pounds of damage was being caused by bombings of commercial property, and established hotels like the Grand Central and the Midland closed down. The Europa, which had been built on the site of the railway station in Great Victoria Street, right beside the Grand Opera House, had an inimitable claim to fame as the most-bombed building in Europe. It kept going, and was the centre for journalists from the international press, but the Grand Opera House naturally shared a lot of the damage, and by 1973 the chairman of the Arts Council, Dr Stanley Worrall, considered the theatre was 'so scathed that no major touring companies can be accommodated there'. Funding and support were channelled less to Belfast and more to smaller centres throughout Northern Ireland.

Amid the gloom strong lights were burning. In 1967 the first steps had been taken towards the establishment of a festival at Queen's University under the directorship of Michael Emerson, and this continued without interruption for the next two decades. Michael Emerson would be succeeded as festival director by Michael Barnes.

The 1960s had seen the emergence of a vigorous interest in Northern Ireland's legacy of buildings, and the Ulster Architectural Heritage Society was set up, largely inspired and led by the Belfast solicitor C.E.B. Brett. Charles Brett had published the influential book on the architecture of the city, *Buildings of Belfast 1700–1914,* in 1967, although it has to be said that his reference to the Grand Opera House is very scant, and in his revised edition of 1985 he writes, 'Here I must acknowledge my failure to appreciate the merits of the Grand Opera House. . . . today I would certainly accord the building three stars.' Even Hugh Dixon's assessment of the building in his definitive work *An Introduction to Ulster Architecture,* published in 1975, is just a little apologetic for the very Victorianism of the theatre:

> Some late Victorian buildings are so elaborate externally as to appear ostentatious and vulgar. But such excesses indoors can produce opulent richness and enjoyable gaiety. . . . The exterior which has suffered some unsympathetic remodelling is interesting rather than exciting. Inside, however, there is an atmosphere of exotic abandon. Decoration is lavished everywhere, from the panelled columns of the pit to the plaster framework of the ceiling paintings. Balcony fronts, heavy with vegetable relief and oriental goddesses, sway between columns mounted with elephants' heads. Layers of boxes with gilt frames and velvet hangings rise to roofs with onion domes.

The Ulster Architectural Heritage Society had campaigned strongly for the statutory listing of buildings of architectural merit in Northern Ireland, and after this victory had been gained the Grand Opera House, shabby, boarded-up and battered as it was, was the first Belfast building to be listed in 1974. Now at least, the theatre had been granted a little time, and the Arts Council was able to commission a survey of the building from the architect Robert McKinstry.

The survival of Victorian buildings is now recognised as essential to the heart of Belfast, and since 1972 one after another important building of that era has been saved, restored or transformed. The old Public Baths in Ormeau Avenue, McCausland Warehouse in Victoria Street, the Water Office in Donegall Square, the Palm House in Botanic Gardens, the Gas Works and St George's Market – all played an intrinsic part in the history of Belfast, and all have been subjects of campaigns for preservation. One of the most complete rescue and restoration jobs was the miraculous survival of the Crown Liquor Saloon, a high-Victorian public house of the same period as the Grand Opera House, and sitting just across the road in Great

Victoria Street. The National Trust took over the pub in 1976, the London committees and staff of the trust accepting the merits of this most unusual of National Trust properties in a gesture of generosity and confidence in the work of the Northern Ireland committee.

With listing, the survival of the Grand Opera House building seemed assured, but not the survival of the theatre. It was by the smallest possible margin in a vote at a meeting of the Arts Council that the council's members, with a capital grant of £168,000, took their courage in their hands, turned their backs on the lure of proposing an expensive modern building, and in 1976 bought the Victorian Grand Opera House from the developer, 'thus holding out the prospect of an appropriate home' for visits by major companies. The auditorium would be restored to its former decorative state, and backstage facilities would incorporate the latest technology. The aesthetic qualities of the theatre itself were not of prime importance, as the Arts Council said:

The decision to rehabilitate the Grand Opera House has not been taken on sentimental grounds: it would cost at least two and a half million pounds to build a new theatre with comparable opportunities, and in the present climate it is unrealistic to expect the Government to embark upon such a project.

In 1978, Graham Patterson, for the *Daily Telegraph*, covering the Queen's Festival, wrote an article entitled 'Flak jackets and evening dress'. In it he painted a picture of Belfast as an uninviting place for the visitor. 'In the city centre people hurry through the empty streets. Cinema queues are sparse. The Army's presence becomes more noticeable as darkness falls.' The journalist paid tribute to the enthusiasm and persistence of arts administrators in Belfast, and quoted Leo Forte, chairman of the Northern Ireland Opera Trust. 'What was really encouraging was that at our last season people started wearing long dresses and dinner jackets again – it's a little thing, I know, but it's a long time since we saw that in Belfast.' The journalist saw that the survivors in the arts in Ulster were now being rewarded with lavish government spending:

By the time the Grand Opera House had been taken over by developers in the 1970s, Matcham's sumptuous surroundings had degenerated to the mundane.
MONUMENTS AND BUILDINGS RECORD

An ambitious building programme for theatres and community arts centres is going ahead, which will undoubtedly be the envy of their struggling counterparts on the mainland.

The most grandiose scheme is the rebuilding, at a cost of around £1.5m, of Belfast's Grand Opera House. Lacking a large, properly equipped theatre, touring ballet, opera and repertory companies have stayed away. The new 1,100 seat theatre, it is hoped, will end Belfast's cultural isolation.

It would be wrong, however, to picture the arts helping to heal the wounds of the past few years. Ulster will not be transformed by a new theatre. Lord Melchett, the young Minister of State at the Northern Ireland Office, to whom goes most of the credit for the sharp increase in Government spending on the arts, quickly emphasises that they are not a panacea for the Province's deeper problems. 'It is very easy to claim that helping the arts is justified both in itself and because it brings pleasure and happiness to people. But that is too facile.'

But the arts are especially important to the Northern Irish because they prove that their country has another side to the images of violence, hate and destruction which the rest of the world sees.

Although the Labour government, of which Lord Melchett was a member, held the purse strings and was exceptionally open-handed to Northern Ireland in many ways at this period, Sir Charles Brett gives much credit for the foresighted rescue funding for the Grand Opera House to the then permanent secretary of the Department of Education, Arthur Brooke.

So the Grand Opera House was saved as a building, and saved as a theatre: saved as a building by enthusiasm and as a theatre by a mixture of pragmatism and opportunity. But few of those who supported its revival could have foreseen the impact the restoration of the theatre would make on the centre of Belfast.

OUR NED

"I suppose without Maggie's cuts in the construction industry, we could have had whole elephants"

Cartoon in *Project* magazine, September 1980, reflects the effect of Margaret Thatcher's economic policy on the construction industry

8
'AN ACT OF FAITH'

R OBERT MCKINSTRY, commissioned by the Arts Council to carry out an architectural survey of the Grand Opera House, began work in May 1975. His account of his first entry into the theatre is evocative:

With memories going back to childhood and Christmas pantomimes in the late Thirties, I had expected a deep plunge into waves of nostalgia. What struck me much more was the extraordinarily abandoned look of the inside, as if everybody had suddenly quit the theatre in a great hurry. The house manager's black jacket still hung on the back of his office door, the ashtrays attached to the seats had never been emptied, and in the bar there were still half-full glasses and crates of bottled beer. It was like the *Marie Celeste*. Apart from the general neglect and the air of total surrender, the inevitable wood rot, the mess of the Glengall Street dressing rooms where bomb blasts from the nearby Europa Hotel had damaged the roof, and the deep pool of water in the orchestra pit where the permanent pumping system no longer functioned, the building, particularly the auditorium, was found to be in a rather better condition than we had expected. The only exception was the foundations where the tops of the timber piles supporting the ground beams had rotted. The list of building defects was long but not catastrophic, and we reported that the Grand Opera House could be satisfactorily repaired, restored and upgraded to present-day standards.

When permission for the work to go ahead was finally given, the contractors appointed to the job were H. & J. Martin, the company that had built

Robert McKinstry, architect of the restoration scheme, 1975–80
GRAND OPERA HOUSE

Opposite:
The restored auditorium of the Grand Opera House
MONUMENTS AND BUILDINGS RECORD

the original theatre in 1895. To build the theatre from scratch had taken them just one year; starting in 1976 its restoration took them just under four years to complete.

The first priority was to make the building wind- and water-tight and to eradicate rot, with the insertion of new slating and leadwork, and appropriate windows. A major difficulty lay in redressing the problems caused by changes in the watertable, which with the failure of the pump had resulted in the flooding of the area below the stage. The recapping of the timber piles of the foundations was one of the slowest parts of the job, as no mechanical diggers could be brought in and all the painstaking and laborious dirty work had to be done by hand with spades, as indeed it would have been done eighty-one years before. Robert McKinstry described the scene:

During a hot summer it was as if a dozen or more gravediggers were at work in cold water-logged vaults. When the excavations moved into the auditorium I experienced for the first time the sharp surrealist clash of mud and rough concrete cheek by jowl with gilt and plush. It soon became a familiar sight.

The level of the water, and the generally aqueous nature of the job, led to one story that several original piles were covered in barnacles.

To provide the technical requirements of a modern theatre Robert McKinstry worked with the specialist theatre consultant Anthony Easterbrook of John Wyckham Associates. The size of the stage of the theatre was considered adequate, if not generous, but the real difficulties lay in the cramped capacity in the wings, a problem that the limited site of the theatre made intractable. One solution employed was to create further opportunities to 'fly' scenery by raising the roof of the stage by twenty feet and replacing the old timber fly grid with a new steel grid and fly gallery, and a new double purchase system of counterweights. Some very successful productions, designed especially for the Grand Opera House, have taken full advantage of the extra flexibility the fly system gives. Opera Northern Ireland, for example, always finds extreme difficulty in operating two productions which are presented on alternate nights, because of the necessity of storing the scenery between productions. The fly system has been a boon in these circumstances, and the company has

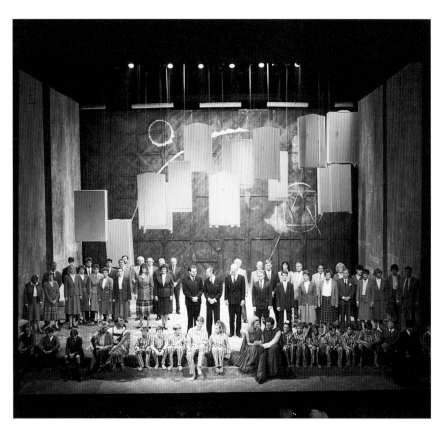

Opera Northern Ireland always struggles with problems of cramped space in the wings. The 1990 production of *The Magic Flute* used a set largely composed of 'flying wardrobes' to great effect.
JILL JENNINGS,
CHRISTOPHER HILL PHOTOGRAPHIC

been able to present imaginatively designed operas using this system. A celebrated production of *The Magic Flute*, directed by Clare Venables and designed by Tim Reed, took the concept one stage further and used dozens of 'flying wardrobes' to illustrate the opera in an enchanting, innovative and highly successful way.

Opera has also benefited from the increased space afforded to the orchestra by Robert McKinstry's extension of the height of the basement, which had been five and a half feet, by lowering the floor by two feet and creating a decently sized orchestra pit to accommodate sixty players, complete with band room and conductor's room. Principal and chorus dressing rooms were extended and brought up to standard, and became capable of accommodating up to eighty people, a generous allowance for most large-scale extravaganzas, although in the 'flying wardrobe' production of Opera Northern Ireland's *Magic Flute*, the additional hundred or so young actors and actresses from the Royal Belfast Academical Institution and St Louise's Comprehensive College had to make a costumed dash from the nearby Ulster Unionist Party headquarters in Glengall Street in order to make their very effective contribution to the operas.

It was in a way fortunate that the most dilapidated and damaged areas of the building were the areas where essential upgrading to high technical specification was required, so there was no conflict between preservation and modernisation.

The front of the house, and the all-important auditorium, provided a different challenge. The structure of the building was comparatively unscathed, the original architect's work was still integral to the building, if not completely intact, and any renewal had to include a strong commitment to the Victorian design. In his handling of the front of the house, Robert McKinstry had a very clear idea of his concept:

> In the refurbishing of nineteenth-century theatres an obsession with faithful restoration and too strong an urge to re-create what once was can easily result in a museum-like atmosphere or else a cardboard musical comedy world on the wrong side of the proscenium arch. I have become aware, too, that a heavily ornate gilt and plush auditorium – no matter how charming – can appear oppressive in these times and too redolent of a social hierarchy. But the fact that, in the Opera House today, everyone comes into the same entrance hall, all foyers inter-communicate and the stall seating can be removed for local 'prom concert' events should make theatre-going much more relaxing.

Protective covers shroud the auditorium while restoration work is in progress
MONUMENTS AND BUILDINGS RECORD

Robert McKinstry's sure touch in capturing the feel of the period and combining it with an engaging and welcoming opulence together with practical considerations was admired by Sir Charles Brett:

> The auditorium is the most important part of the building. It has everything a theatre should have: excellent sightlines from every part of the house, though the number of seats has been reduced from the original 2,500, largely accommodated on hard benches in the gods, to 1,050, all now in comfortable seats of traditional pattern; efficient ventilation; outstandingly good acoustics; and above all, as the architect says, 'a sense of the exotic and an atmosphere of magic'. . . . Everywhere is red velvet, plush, and gilt – and it is one of the triumphs of this restoration that the fresh gilding, instead of being clamorous and strident, has somehow been imbued overnight with an Edwardian patina.

The 'new' painted ceiling: no visual evidence existed for restoration purposes, so artist Cherith McKinstry had to rely on descriptions, 1895 newspaper reports, personal memories, and her own creativity.
MONUMENTS AND BUILDINGS RECORD

One of the most difficult elements of the renewal of the theatre to get exactly right was the restoration of the ceiling. There was no trace, apart from the descriptions in the contemporary press, of the six large ceiling paintings, and Robert McKinstry described the frustration of having some knowledge of the subjects portrayed, but no photographic evidence:

> I can just remember as a child seeing the six painted ceiling panels described so vividly in the early newspaper reports. I recall a blue sky with stars above the oriental balcony with its little potted palms. Then I was told of garlands of roses hanging from the balcony and of the inevitable putti. It is tantalising that no photographs of the original painted ceiling exist and I spent many months searching for a modern painter who might re-create this scene without resorting to a slick pastiche of cherubs and roses like a Valentine, or the crude naivety of a fairground booth.

Three artists submitted sketches for consideration by the Arts Council, and Cherith McKinstry was chosen, to great effect, as she was to achieve a seamless harmony of style, mood, content and colour.

The enchantment and integrity of the treatment of the interior – 'dramatic and magical', as Robert McKinstry put it – softened any cries of protest from the purists at the one concession to change, which was the addition of a crush bar, cantilevered out over the pavement into Great Victoria Street. The problem to be solved was once again the extreme physical limitations of the site and the need to provide the facilities required for a comfortable and amiable evening's entertainment. Although this addition represented a visually inescapable alteration to the front of the building, it was handled with the same sensitivity and attention to detail that was so successful inside. Robert McKinstry wanted the new foyer extension to look 'like a modern version of a Victorian conservatory much as Matcham himself built over the front entrance to his Theatre Royal in Portsmouth'. The new architect also pointed to the advantages which the new bar would provide for the patrons of the 1980s:

> May I also say that behind this new extension the original brick external wall and the cast-stone decoration around the original three centre windows still remain but now two of the windows have become archways into the new extension and the central bay has been built. In fact when you are enjoying a drink at this bar you can also have a splendid close up view of Matcham's sculptural decoration – a view only the window cleaners previously enjoyed.

The same attention to detail and the quality of material used throughout the theatre add enormously to the pleasure and sense of occasion that theatre-goers enjoy. From gleaming brass to thick carpets, from polished wood to stained glass, from thoughtfully designed drink shelves to appropriate fittings in the lavatories, the theatre has been designed to welcome, accommodate and cosset its patrons.

The new 'conservatory style' crush bar – the only major alteration to the façade and front of house in Robert McKinstry's restoration scheme
MONUMENTS AND BUILDINGS RECORD

An aesthetically satisfying and technically efficient theatre was now virtually achieved. The funding came, spasmodically at times and stage by stage, but it came. It now remained for the management and the artistic policy of the Grand Opera House to be established. Four key members of staff were appointed in 1980. The first was Michael Barnes, who became general manager and artistic director. Initially he was seconded for two years by Queen's University, where he had been a history lecturer, and where he had established a reputation as a vigorous, innovative and attuned director of the Belfast Festival at Queen's. As artistic director, Michael Barnes had many great strengths. He had a breadth of knowledge and vision, a love of classical music and drama and the ability to accrue expertise. Staff speak warmly of his loyalty. He had a relentless optimism, sometimes in the face of seemingly impossible odds and, once he had fixed his eye on a target, a tenacity of purpose. He was undeniably successful in bringing perhaps reluctant artistes and companies to a troubled city, and his stubborn refusal to be deflected from an idea with which he had become enamoured resulted in some notable coups, especially in the visits of the

Grand Opera House general manager and artistic director Michael Barnes and the figure of Mercury, which was reinstated at the corner of the theatre, August 1980

BELFAST TELEGRAPH

Hamburg and Royal Swedish ballets, for which he enlisted support from the highest levels.

Michael Barnes quickly became an instantly recognisable figure on the streets of Belfast. One story he himself enjoys telling relates an evening spent with distinguished impresarios in the Europa Hotel. During the evening the guests won a large side of salmon, and knowing that they had to travel back to London, gave it to their host. With the large side of salmon under his arm, Barnes left the hotel and got into a waiting taxi with the instruction, 'Festival House, please.' It was then that one of the men in the front seat turned round and said, 'I'm sorry, Mr Barnes, this is a police car.'

Around him a seemingly disparate but ultimately extremely cohesive core of staff was appointed. John Branch was made general manager. Trained as a scientist and formerly a manager in the industrial liaison unit of Queen's, he was subsequently involved with a research project with the Arts Council, and was a constant steady presence at the theatre, calm and competent. The job of technical manager was given to John Jordan. A native of Ballymoney, his credentials, which included ten years' experience with the Royal Opera House, Covent Garden, were impeccable, and he has remained with the Grand Opera House ever since, contributing a rare degree of experience and expertise. Robert Agnew, a languages graduate from Trinity College, Dublin, had worked in the textile industry before following his intuition and the arts to become an intelligent communicator as publicity and press officer. He went on to become acting director of Queen's Festival. The job of finding other technical members of staff proved difficult. Because of the size of the theatre it should have been important to have experienced members of staff in a number of different roles. However, when the curtain rose on the first night of the restored Grand Opera House, 15 September 1980, there were, in fact, very few experienced professionals in the house.

John Jordan had gathered together a stage crew within weeks of the season opening. He says it was literally a matter of teaching from scratch: 'This is downstage, this is stage left, we call this a tab, we call this a follow spot.' By the gala performance everything was more or less in place, but when John Jordan was asked by Sean Rafferty how it had all gone, he replied, in typical vein, 'Only my laundry man will ever know.'

In May 1979, the Arts Council had announced the names of the members of the Grand Opera House committee. Paddy Brand, a well-known businessman with a keen interest in the arts, was chairman. He was joined by Shane Belford, a former architect who was currently development director of the Northern Ireland Tourist Board, a body that had been a leading player in urging the restoration of the theatre. Fionnuala Cook, the lady mayoress, who also had experience of working with the Lyric Theatre, RTE and the Project Art Gallery, Dublin; Robert Coulter, controller of BBC Scotland; Dr Maurice Hayes, who was then senior assistant secretary at the Department of Health and Social Services and a member of several arts-related bodies; Dr Peter Jupp, senior lecturer at Queen's University and a key player in the development of the Belfast Festival at Queen's; John Knipe, who had extensive experience in the field of amateur drama; and Arthur Brooke, the civil servant who had been so influential in securing the initial grant for the theatre (who had agreed to become a member of the trust after his retirement), were the other members of the board.

In May 1979, too, the Grand Opera House committee had declared its future policy and plans. Its intention was to offer a wide range of major events, to cater for as many different tastes as possible and to attract a wide variety of people through the theatre's doors. The theatre programme would include events in such fields as opera, operetta and musicals, ballet and dance, drama both light and serious, shows featuring stars from the world of popular entertainment, and events for children. The stated ambition was to attract events of very high professional quality, although there would still be room for amateur productions of appropriate size and scale. While the Grand Opera House would not have its own resident company it was possible that occasional productions might be specially mounted, and it was hoped that a pantomime could be produced in this way. In short, take away a circus and add a ballet and the artistic programmes for the Grand Opera House in 1980 and 1895 were not so very different. J.F. Warden would have been proud of the way the reopening of the Grand Opera House was stage-managed. Anticipation began as the building work progressed. As the hoardings came down and the newly restored building was revealed, the eagerness of anticipation heightened. Then a date was given for the grand opening night, but no details of the programme. A newspaper headline spoke of a 'mystery gala'. Potential guests began to wonder if they would be in the audience. A book and an exhibition of the work of the theatre's original architect, Frank Matcham, were in the making.

Then there was drama, as an accidental fire held back building work. Finally, on 15 September 1980, the gala night arrived. The privileged audience consisted of leading figures in the arts and civic life, politicians and civil servants. There were also the people who had worked on the restoration of the theatre, and some who had been associated with it through some of the most significant moments of its history. One example was John McBride, who came with his wife Pat. He had appeared in the Ulster Literary Theatre's *The Drone* fifty years before, and he confessed to being extremely moved by the reopening.

Those who accepted the invitation received a card that very much

Michael Barnes and the full cast
on stage at the gala night reopening
of the Grand Opera House,
15 September 1980
GRAND OPERA HOUSE

reflected the tone of the evening:

> We are happy that you are attending the Gala Re-Opening and hope that you
> will have a specially enjoyable time on this happy occasion.
>
> We are keeping the full programme of the Gala Performance as a surprise,
> but you may like to know that we shall be touching on a whole variety of the
> performing arts and that a number of most distinguished Ulster artists have
> kindly agreed to perform on this very special night. . . . As you will have
> noted on the invitation, dress is optional on this occasion. We know that
> there will undoubtedly be some people who would prefer to dress formally,
> but our chief concern is that everyone should dress as they wish and we are
> happy to leave this to your own judgement.

In fact, Michael Barnes achieved a programme for the opening gala that
perfectly mirrored the history of the theatre. The best of Ulster talent was
there to play its part, and the evening was handled with the style, gusto,
and great affection that were to characterise the succeeding programmes
and the relationship of the theatre with its city. The evening began with a
flourish – a striking, specially composed fanfare – followed by a prologue
read by actor Colin Blakely. The Ulster Orchestra was in the pit for the first
time, under the baton of Dr Havelock Nelson who had done so much for
the development of music in Northern Ireland. Heather Harper sang
exquisitely, drawing on operatic works, including 'Vissi d'Arte' by Puccini,
and Uel Deane dipped into nostalgia with Tosti's 'Parted' and 'Roses of

Picardy', as well as joining with Mary Gilmore to resurrect the old favourite, 'Maritana', while the Ulster Operatic Company kept reminders of the good old days to the front with an arrangement of popular numbers including 'Dolly Gray', in which the audience was invited to participate. London Festival Ballet contributed to the evening too, continuing its long-established relationship with the theatre, Frank Carson brought his own inimitable style of humour, and that doyen of the spoken word Denys Hawthorne maintained the theme of nostalgia with his recitation of 'The Green Eye of the Yellow God'. It was a splendid and appropriate evening.

Michael Barnes (left) with Colin Blakely in the dressing room at the gala reopening, 15 September 1980
GRAND OPERA HOUSE

Amidst the triumph and celebration of the evening, however, a small dark shadow of reality crossed over the stage. Dr Stanley Worrall, chairman of the Arts Council for Northern Ireland, made a speech that in the context of the evening was sensational. In it he laid on the line the fact that the Arts Council for Northern Ireland had probably overreached itself in taking on the Grand Opera House, and that the future of the theatre might be unsustainable. He made reference to the fact that the oral promise of a government subsidy for the Grand Opera House would not now be kept. He clearly looked to government ministers Humphrey Atkins and Lord Elton, sitting in the audience, not to leave the Arts Council in the unacceptable position of having to deprive other recipients of grants in order to underpin the £1,000 per day funding which the theatre required. In the prevailing economic climate the opening of the Grand Opera House was, Dr Worrall said, 'an act of faith'. And, not for the first time in its history, the onus of the future of the theatre was seen to lie in the hands of its audience. Dr Worrall did not mince his words as he turned to the audience. 'The Opera House will be open when you want it, only if you support it regularly.'

The editorial of the *Belfast Telegraph* took up the theme:

> The re-opening of the Grand Opera House in Belfast is not only the rebirth of a magnificent theatre but also a landmark in the life of this province and its capital city.
>
> Despite the beauty, the gaiety and the sense of occasion last night, there was a large cloud on the horizon. Dr Stanley Worrall, chairman of the Arts Council who are the proprietors of the theatre, spelt out the harsh economic realities. . . . There is no point in crying 'Shame' like some members of last night's audience. The arts as well as industry, commerce and other sectors of British society have to face economic facts. It is right that the arts should be subsidised but the question now is how can the available money be put to the best use.
>
> It is clear that without strong public support the Grand Opera House will face severe financial difficulties. . . . The re-opening is indeed an act of faith but it is up to everyone on both sides of the footlights to ensure that the brightness continues.

Heather Harper, Northern Ireland's most celebrated soprano, who sang at the gala night reopening, 15 September 1980
GRAND OPERA HOUSE

The first season under Michael Barnes's guidance was a huge success on nearly every count. A varied programme left no room for jibes of elitism, and sell-out followed sell-out. The anarchic comedian Rowan Atkinson, long before he had become identified with Blackadder and Mr Bean, preceded the smooth-voiced and very popular singer Val Doonican. Backstage staff got used to being close to famous faces. Rowan Atkinson was found to be 'extremely shy', and Val Doonican the 'sweetest man', just like his rocking-chair-and-cardigan image. Robert Agnew found that selling the shows was pushing against an open door. Everyone wanted to go to the Grand Opera House. Agnew had just one problem with the opening season. The principal actress in *Le Cirque Imaginaire*, an extraordinary production for which the Belfast technical staff had to round up tame farmyard animals, refused to let it be known that she was Charlie Chaplin's daughter, which was asking a lot of any publicist.

Brian Friel, whose play *Translations*, performed by the Field Day Theatre Company, was a landmark production in the reopened Grand Opera House's first season
FIELD DAY

The Northern Ireland Opera Trust returned triumphantly to its rightful stage with a *Tosca* for which every seat was sold, and one of the most significant events of the year was the arrival, early in the season, of the Field Day Theatre Company with Brian Friel's *Translations*. Field Day was a new company, based in Derry, founded that year by Friel and others, and 'like the Irish Literary Theatre, a concept, not a building', according to D.E.S. Maxwell, who defined its role as a theatre company 'which seeks new plays canvassing the turbulence of present-day Ireland and its informing past'. *Translations* has been seen as a milestone in twentieth-century drama in its use of the historical details of the 1833 period during which Irish place names were anglicised to examine the tensions of political and cultural relationships through the story of personal tragedies. Its cast list was impressive, billing Ray McAnally, Liam Neeson and Stephen Rea.

The first pantomime to be staged at the Grand Opera House since 1971 surpassed all expectations; it was an in-house production of *Cinderella* in which Frank Carson revelled in the role of Buttons. Attendances averaged a remarkable 97 per cent, and by Christmas there was no doubt that the Belfast public had voted overwhelmingly in favour of this new asset to their city.

Not quite so well attended were the Abbey Theatre's production of Friel's *Faith Healer*, and the Centaur Theatre of Montreal's *Balconville* by Fenmarlo, which was one of the most ambitious productions ever shown in the Grand Opera House – with a huge set of apartment blocks on two levels, a unique drama of real scale, and spoken in French-Canadian. With the energetic musical *Ipi Tombi*, plus Agatha Christie, Cole Porter and Shakespeare, however, the average house for the first six months stood at a more than satisfactory 88 per cent.

In that first season, though, a few problems did begin to emerge. Costs for bringing in touring companies, and the expenses of security and insurance, proved to be much higher than anticipated. In addition, the volatile security situation in the city proved too much of a deterrent for several shows. The comedy *Make or Break*, a celebrity concert by Julian Bream and the Northern Ballet Theatre were all cancelled, so it was clear that although the opening of the Grand Opera House was a bold statement, its success was still unproven.

After the huge popularity of the first season, the following decade showed a steady pattern of attendance by the Belfast public. It was not long before the ever-popular *Joseph and the Amazing Technicolor Dreamcoat* made its first visit to the Grand Opera House; this was a show that would continue to fill houses year after year, its engaging blend of music, colour and story proving an irresistible magnet for Belfast audiences. Very often the same patrons would return for the same shows time after time. The booking office staff had become used to supporters returning week after week to the same seats. Now they became used to them coming night after night.

One night, however, the disaster that every theatre manager fears struck:

The musical *Ipi Tombi*, a box-office success in the first season of the reopened Grand Opera House
GRAND OPERA HOUSE

Joseph and the Amazing Technicolor Dreamcoat played to capacity houses in the Grand Opera House in June 1981, and returned to hugely enthusiastic audiences, year after year, during the 1980s.

GRAND OPERA HOUSE

in the middle of *Joseph*, the theatre suffered its one and only power cut since reopening. Because the show was so popular, there was no question of offering the audience alternative seats on another night, so John Jordan found a single candle that had been used in a recent production and the cast came to the front of the stage and sat, feet dangling over the edge, and sang their way through the songs to piano accompaniment until the lights came on again. The show, the only one in Belfast to survive the power cut, finished at about midnight. The audience had had a great time; it was another Grand Opera House party.

When Scottish Ballet brought *Romeo and Juliet* in 1982–83, it was the first full-length ballet to have been seen in Belfast for twenty years. The company continued to bring a range of productions to the Grand Opera House; they included *Giselle*, *The Nutcracker*, *Swan Lake*, *Carmen* and *Peter Pan*. Its *Peter Pan* was wonderfully memorable, with a flying ballet which combined magic and grace.

It was at this time that a familiar and colourful personality became an unmissable presence at the great Grand Opera House events. Charles Fitzgerald, the *News Letter* critic, often dressed in hunting pink or midnight blue and regularly sporting a cloak or a buttonhole, began his habit of throwing flowers from his box on the final night of the ballet or opera. Deeply moved by the significance of the visits by the Scottish companies, with whom he had a long-standing association, and by the quality of their productions, he asserted that the tribute of flowers was as fitting in Belfast as it would be in any European opera house.

In November 1984, in an extraordinary and powerful combination, the Chieftains linked with the Irish National Ballet to produce *The Playboy of the Western World*. A year later, Northern Ballet came to Belfast with *A Midsummer Night's Dream*, and often as part of the Belfast Festival at Queen's major European companies, including the Royal Flanders Ballet and the Royal Swedish Ballet, visited the theatre. In 1985 the Royal Swedish Ballet came specifically to Belfast, not as part of a tour, and although this presented more logistical problems than usual, it also offered the managements of both the theatre and the ballet company the freedom to choose repertoire. Grand Opera House audiences enjoyed first a triple bill of Act 2 of *La Bayadère*, *Before Nightfall* and *The Rite of Spring*, followed by a sumptuous production of *The Sleeping Beauty*. The Ulster Orchestra played for the Royal Swedish Ballet, and a splendid visit was capped by the attendance of the company's patron, Princess Christina of Sweden. The Hamburg Ballet brought another triumph with a staging of *A Midsummer Night's Dream* that many remember as being 'out of this world'. Dance of a different genre was presented by Wayne Sleep; appearing in *Bits and Pieces*, this famous dancer seduced the audience with the astonishing eloquence of his movement.

Maeve Largy and Mark Frizell, dancers with the Patricia Mulholland School of Dancing, are seen here with Sally Collard-Gentle, with whom they made their debut in Scottish Ballet's *Giselle* in May 1983.
BELFAST TELEGRAPH

It was to prove harder to bring touring opera to Belfast. Scottish Opera brought *La Traviata* and a simply excellent *Eugene Onegin*, produced by David Pountney and with a first-rate Scottish Opera company including Malcolm Donnelly, Linda Ormiston, Nelly Miricioiu, and Alan Oke. Scottish Opera was later able to bring *La Traviata*, *The Bartered Bride* and *The Barber of Seville*, and Wexford Festival Opera brought a rarely performed Mozart work *Zaïde*. With considerable astuteness, Michael Barnes highlighted on the season's brochure an attractive and very promising young singer, taking the role of Zaïde, whom he had seen at Wexford. She

'The Peasants' Chorus' from Scottish Opera's production of *Eugene Onegin*; although Scottish Opera was able to tour to Belfast at the beginning of the 1980s, the costs to the Grand Opera House soon became prohibitive.
SCOTTISH OPERA

was then twenty-five years old, and her name was Lesley Garrett.

Finances have always been a major problem in the staging of opera, and by 1985 it had become so expensive to tour an opera company that Michael Barnes conceded it had finally become apparent that the Grand Opera House could no longer afford to support even one short week of touring opera.

However, Opera Northern Ireland continued to fly the flag for opera locally, presenting productions of a quality that drew the handsome praise of many of the critics of the London-based papers. Under the creative and musical direction of Kenneth Montgomery, an Ulsterman who had gained a considerable reputation in Europe and America, and with another Ulsterman, Randall Shannon, as general manager, the company was able to mount two seasons of opera in a year. Although many names familiar to Covent Garden and opera houses throughout the world came to sing in Opera Northern Ireland productions, it specialised in finding young international up-and-coming singers, as well as in ensuring that a platform for the best of Ulster's emigrant singers was available. Notable among the successes Opera Northern Ireland presented at the Grand Opera House were Richard Strauss's *Ariadne auf Naxos*, directed by Derryman Seamus McGrenera, a *Marriage of Figaro* set in a twentieth-century Irish country

house and directed by Tim Coleman, and a powerful *Faust* directed by Bliss Hebert. Among local professional singers who appeared with Opera Northern Ireland were Kate McCarney, Angela Feeney, Bruno Caproni and Michael Neill.

Kenneth Montgomery achieved an ambition in completing a Mozart cycle of opera in the theatre. Surprisingly, throughout its history, the operas of Mozart had been very rarely performed in the Grand Opera House, although Montgomery held that the acoustics and intimacy of the Grand Opera House perfectly suited operas like *Così fan tutte* and *The Magic Flute*. He is eloquent about the fact that a great delight of Matcham's theatre is the close relationship of the audience to the players, and the response that the players or singers are able to make to that relationship. An advocate of the importance of casting singers who can act and who look convincing in their roles, he relished conducting Mozart in an auditorium in which singers could do full justice to the subtlety of Mozart by their close contact with the audience. When Opera Northern Ireland played the Mozart cycle, Belfast audiences did full justice to these operas in their support and attendance.

One evening, when conducting *Die Entführung aus dem Serail*, Montgomery was surprised by the fervour of applause for the aria by

Tatiana's birthday party from Scottish Opera's production of *Eugene Onegin*
SCOTTISH OPERA

The harlequinade from Opera
Northern Ireland's *Ariadne
auf Naxos*, a celebrated
production at the Grand Opera
House at the beginning of
Kenneth Montgomery's term
as artistic director
OPERA NORTHERN IRELAND

Frederick Vassar as Mephistopheles
in Opera Northern Ireland's outstanding production of *Faust*,
which was performed at the
Grand Opera House in 1989
OPERA NORTHERN IRELAND

Opera Northern Ireland's
production of *The Magic Flute*,
September 1990:
Left: Rosemary Joshua
and Geoffrey Dolton
Below: Geoffrey Dolton
OPERA NORTHERN IRELAND

Pedrillo. Backstage he pondered the reason for this. 'Did you not hear the bang?' he was asked. It turned out that a bomb had exploded very close to the theatre, beside the Assembly Building, in the middle of Pedrillo's aria, the words of which, translated on surtitles above the proscenium, are 'Only cowards are afraid.'

Some orchestras have pointed out drawbacks in the conditions in the pit of the Grand Opera House. Kenneth Montgomery acknowledges that there are difficulties. 'It is an "analytical" pit. There is no "bloom", and so players have to be extremely accurate, which is, of course, a very good thing.' He was less forgiving of the conductor's room, tucked in at a very low level behind the stage. When the theatre was first restored, some connection to the sewers of Belfast left uncovered made it a less than agreeable space to occupy, and the stage manager's habit of leaving a collection of his shoes there did not make matters any better. In 1993 after a bomb attack badly damaged the theatre, the problem of the sewer was rectified, although it still remains a stuffy, dark little space.

Tenor Carlo Bergonzi receives a standing ovation after his recital at the Grand Opera House in April 1981
GRAND OPERA HOUSE

Music of very different kinds found a place at the Grand Opera House. The Berlin Chamber Orchestra brought its superb classical musicianship, whilst a memorable concert of quite another type was given by the great tenor Carlo Bergonzi, who endeared himself to audience and staff alike, was entirely charming, received a standing ovation, and appeared to enjoy himself thoroughly.

An undoubted highlight was the first concert that demonstrated the unrivalled supremacy of Van Morrison, perhaps the most evocative of the wide spectrum of musicians who played on the Grand Opera House stage during the 1980s. So many people remember the Van Morrison concerts of the time, the emotion and enthusiasm engendered by the return of that best-loved Belfast star to sing the songs of the streets of the city – 'Cyprus Avenue' and 'Cleaning Windows'. A generation existed in Belfast that had grown up with Van Morrison, that remembered him playing at Inst dances and at Queen's and at Sammy Houston's. These people had identified with the excitement, raw strength and rebellion of his band Them, and through the electric, vital harmony of 'Here Comes the Night', 'Brown-Eyed Girl' and 'Gloria' they had matured with him to the 'Bright Side of the Road', 'Into the Mystic' and 'Beautiful Vision'. Those who followed his music with love regretted the fact that he had not been home since 1967, and that he had gone to Dublin on a tour first, but there was no resentment in the audience, and those who went to the shows describe with feeling how the theatre some-how adapted itself into a night-club, and became an intimate space for a thousand people, a band and one man. Backstage, Grand Opera House staff were impressed by Van Morrison's dedication towards his music. That was his first and last concern. He was a quiet person who wanted his own privacy and expected others to respect that desire. And, for once in its history, a star's visit to the theatre was not completely transitory: the album *Live at the Grand Opera House* was released by Van Morrison in 1984.

The theatre proved surprisingly accommodating to bands and their respective followings, which made up audiences unlike many of the other packed houses. The Grand Opera House rocked to the music of Fairport Convention and the Hothouse Flowers, to the stamping of feet and dancing in the aisles. In one of his first ventures into the world of concerts, Michael Barnes had booked the Communards, and by good luck or by good judgement their visit to Belfast coincided with their position at number one in the charts, and predictable scenes of rapturous enthusiasm followed. After a successful and essentially good-natured attempt to prevent fans from reaching the stage from the stalls, house manager Eric Reid emerged from the fray with the trousers of his evening suit in tatters.

The big musical always drew enthusiastic audiences. In addition to perennial favourite *Joseph and the Amazing Technicolor Dreamcoat*, audiences flocked to see *Evita* and *Piaf*, and the management noted with satisfaction that it was able to attract a newer, younger audience with a show like *Grease*. The arrival of the big musical marked for many a milestone in the theatre's coming of age. When the cross in *Jesus Christ Superstar* rose majestically to a sound with the power of a Concorde engine and amazing lighting effects, spectators felt they were about to witness something very special. A hefty investment in bringing a lavish production of *The Sound of Music* with Liz Robertson and Christopher Cazenove proved rewarding in both the size of the audiences and the financial success of the show, which would have covered its costs save for the incurred 17.5 per cent VAT. The hugely enjoyable musical *Buddy* features in many people's favourite memories of the theatre as an entertainment which was sheer good fun. It was during this run that the Grand Opera House had to be cleared for a bomb scare – almost incredibly for the only time. It was a challenge for which the staff under Eric Reid was well prepared. A suspected car bomb outside the Europa meant that the audience had to be directed to the left towards Wellington Place. The warning came just as the curtain was about to go up on a full house, but within four minutes the auditorium was empty and the audience was huddled in pouring rain outside the ABC Cinema. Around 9.30 p.m., the police gave the all-clear, and 95 per cent of the audience returned to a great show to which they gave a standing ovation. It was a night to remember.

Local favourites like Phil Coulter came regularly, and there was always room for artistes like Mary Black or Paul Brady. There were occasional individual visitors of great celebrity, like Stephane Grappelli.

Very few big gala performances were complete without Phil Coulter.

Van Morrison played memorable concerts at the Grand Opera House in 1983 – his first concerts in his home town since 1967
CHRISTOPHER HILL PHOTOGRAPHIC

With a huge musical pedigree and a rare combination of knowledge and intuition as to what will succeed musically, his concerts are always well attended. He has a happy knack of mixing the popular with the classical, and there are few throughout the world who will not have heard a Phil Coulter song somewhere, whether it is the almost-ubiquitous Cliff Richard Eurovision Song Contest entry 'Congratulations' or the relaxing, melodious piano arrangements that are considered perfect for in-flight entertainment or setting the right ambiance in a restaurant. The period of the reopening of the theatre coincided with a time when Phil Coulter's band was enjoying vitality and success; the band was a good mixture of attractive young music graduates and experienced session musicians. Touring was great fun and there were fine times to be had.

The classically trained flautist James Galway paid a memorable visit in 1986, in the company of the celebrated Irish traditional musicians the Chieftains. This was a combination of extraordinary chemistry. The audience watched and listened as James Galway, always the mercurial, attractive genius, evidently relished this juxtaposition with geniuses of a different tradition, who were equally demanding of their own excellence but who possessed a musical integrity and generosity of spirit that could embrace a star name without losing any of their own identity.

In complete contrast, when the Moscow Balalaika Orchestra made its visit to the Grand Opera House, the old ways of the USSR were still in play, and two very stern companions accompanied the entourage of two hundred players and management everywhere. At a post-performance reception in the bar of the theatre, at a nod from these two disciplinarians, the party was suddenly over.

Phil Coulter – one of the many Ulster musicians who drew large audiences to the Grand Opera House
DAVID GRAHAM OF HILLSBOROUGH

9

GOLDEN MILE,
GOLDEN MOMENTS

THROUGHOUT THE PERIOD after the reopening of the Grand Opera House, humour was very well represented. The first year saw John Wells's hilarious *Anyone for Dennis?* and highlights of later years included Hinge and Bracket, Dave Allen, Billy Connolly and Dame Edna Everage. Peter Ustinov remained in a class of his own, charming everyone by his consistently humorous and courteous manner, while one-person shows of more serious intent included Prunella Scales as Queen Victoria and Alec McCowen as Kipling. McCowen must have found Matcham's Grand Opera House, built in the heyday of the British Empire, complete with elephants, the ideal setting for his performance. Alec McCowen also brought to the Grand Opera House the Gospel of Mark, which he presented as a narrative. Those who were there on a Sunday afternoon found his interpretation spell-binding; there was rarely an audience whose attention was so captivated. The Grand Opera House had proved itself again to be the perfect vehicle for a variety of performances. In the case of the one-man show, from Micheál Mac Liammóir to Peter Ustinov, it is an excellent place for talking to your friends.

The management of the Grand Opera House was able to maintain a constant flow of popular drama, productions that were brought as part of a tour throughout the UK, often either before or after a West End season. Usually these productions would include a voice or face made familiar through television. A typical example was *Born in the Gardens* in 1983, which had Diana Copeland (*Bless this House*), Peter Byrne (*Dixon of Dock Green*) and Alan Dobie in the cast. Throughout the eighties and nineties household names such as John Nettles (*Bergerac*), Stefan Dennis (Paul from the TV soap *Neighbours*), Mark McManus (Taggart of the TV series of the same name) and Toyah Wilcox (well known in the world of rock music before she embarked on an acting career) may have attracted in a new audience more used to watching television than going to the theatre.

True to the management's stated intentions, shows specially with children in mind were booked for the Grand Opera House, and these were

Toyah Wilcox, star of *Peter Pan* in 1995 – one of a new generation of performers to appear at the Grand Opera House
DAVID GRAHAM OF HILLSBOROUGH

generally very well supported. From popular heroes like *Postman Pat*, *Fireman Sam* and *Paddington Bear* to the *Gingerbread Man*, to more challenging productions such as adaptations of the works of E. Nesbitt, Roald Dahl and C.S. Lewis, these shows brought a special atmosphere to the theatre – and new and often very enthusiastic audiences.

Serious drama was very well catered for, with occasional visits by the Irish Theatre Company, the Royal Exchange, Manchester, and Anthony Quayle's Compass Theatre Company, which toured all over the British Isles and brought popular and gifted actors including Dennis Quilley and

Kate O'Mara in productions ranging from *The Royal Hunt of the Sun* to *King Lear*. There were also regular tours from Dublin's Abbey Theatre Company. Of all the Abbey productions, the play that will remain vividly in most memories is Frank McGuinness's moving treatment of the motives and relationships of the men who fought in the First World War: *Observe the Sons of Ulster Marching Towards the Somme*. Packed houses in 1985 found the poignancy of the Donegal writer's sensitive and generous examination of the Protestant psyche, handled by a gifted Abbey company of actors led by Ray McAnally, and against a

Derek Jacobi's acclaimed performance in *Breaking the Code* came to the Grand Opera House in 1992.
DAVID GRAHAM OF HILLSBOROUGH

backdrop of continuing violence, a very powerful combination. Another Abbey production with enormous power to move and enlighten was the Brian Friel play *Dancing at Lughnasa*, which came to the Grand Opera House in 1992 just before a tour to Australia, and which drew houses of 99 per cent.

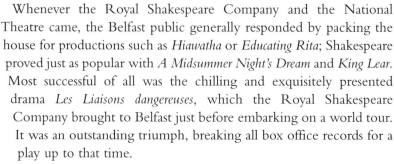

Whenever the Royal Shakespeare Company and the National Theatre came, the Belfast public generally responded by packing the house for productions such as *Hiawatha* or *Educating Rita*; Shakespeare proved just as popular with *A Midsummer Night's Dream* and *King Lear*. Most successful of all was the chilling and exquisitely presented drama *Les Liaisons dangereuses*, which the Royal Shakespeare Company brought to Belfast just before embarking on a world tour. It was an outstanding triumph, breaking all box office records for a play up to that time.

The years under Michael Barnes's directorship saw many such moments. Theatre-goers will not forget strong and moving performances such as Keith Michel's in *Amadeus*, Stephen Rea's in *Making History*, those of Colin Blakely and Dorothy Tutin in the Pinter trilogy *Other Places*, Derek Jacobi's in *Breaking the Code* and the towering portrayal of Richard III by Sir Ian McKellen.

Although *Other Places* was badly supported (as Pinter plays very often are, anywhere), and although it was a very expensive production with three big sets (former staff wince when they think of the cost), members of the management were sure they had been right to bring the trilogy to Belfast, especially as it proved such a fine vehicle for Colin Blakely. The three plays, one set in a taxi depot, one in a hospital ward, and one in a gracious room of an office of a fascist regime where an interrogation is taking place, gave the locally born actor full scope for his sensitive and subtle interpretation, and full play for his flexible and resonant voice. His talents had taken him to a wide range of roles, from Dennis Potter's explosive television play *Son of Man*, to Dr Watson in *Sherlock Holmes*. When Colin Blakely left the ranks of Northern Ireland amateurs to become a professional actor he enjoyed great affection and respect, which remained with him throughout his career.

Spectacularly successful was the visit of Kenneth Branagh's Renaissance Company in 1988. Kenneth Branagh is the Belfast-born actor who had drawn the attention of local audiences through the televised *Billy* trilogy by Graham Reid, which chronicled the life and troubles of a boy growing up in the Belfast of the 1970s. He had won further acclaim through the hugely popular *Fortunes of War* series on television, and the respect of his fellow actors for a career that had been uncompromising in its integrity. With the support of key figures in the profession, in the eighties he launched the theatre company Renaissance with the aim of producing the highest quality classical and modern work in London and the regions 'in as exciting, fresh and entertaining a way as possible, with the very best creative teams available'. Branagh's enthusiasm and commitment drew together an enviable team of directors who were actors – Derek Jacobi for *Hamlet*, Dame Judi Dench for *Much Ado About Nothing* and Geraldine McEwan for *As You Like It*. Branagh himself played Hamlet, Benedick and Touchstone, and for a hot week in June it seemed he could do no wrong for a Belfast audience who simply loved him. In his autobiography *Beginning*, written to subsidise the theatre company, he describes the experience of coming home, and the unanticipated problem of touring sets in theatres of different sizes.

The Opera House, Belfast, and we went from 150 people to 1,000 people. There was a full house. I'd spent all day doing 'local boy makes good' publicity, and in the late afternoon, when I saw our Studio set seemingly adrift in the expanse of the great stage, my heart sank. I was learning quickly that being a small-time impresario and playing Hamlet four times a week was an uneasy mixture. For various reasons, Derek [Jacobi] had not been available to see his show transfer to a big house, and by the time I arrived. . . . stage management and design teams had been working for hours to do an instant conversion. The cast turned up, and although we'd attempted rough re-blockings in the last week at Birmingham, we were faced with immediate adjustments which dealt with sight-line problems that had been impossible to predict in advance. We did what we could on the spot and at seven o'clock I retired to the dressing-room/office I was sharing. . . . Peace seemed very hard to find and this seemed the very best or the very worst preparation for an evening as the moody Dane.

The warm reception from our Belfast audience resolved most of the problems of tiredness and adjustment. They were just plain delighted to see us. After the performance we attended the first of the many parties that would be a feature of the tour, and were often provided by one of the sponsors. . . The reaction of our Belfast hosts was ecstatic, and there, in full and glorious loyalty, were my parents, who had flown over especially to see the great home-coming. They were in danger of expiring with pride.

The bookings for the week ahead were near capacity, there was a great deal of publicity. Walking into town from Uncle Jim and Aunt Kathleen's house, where I was staying during the Belfast run, I was often recognised and stopped. Local people were no longer suspicious of Billy's English accent – they'd read the papers, they'd seen *Fortunes of War* and they now seemed to accept that I was an Ulster one-off. There was a funny sort of inverted snobbery and pride about my involvement with Shakespeare. They liked the idea of one of their lads showing the English how to do it and they were delighted that Belfast was the first stop on the tour. The recurring uneasiness that I felt about my Irishness was beginning to disappear. Suddenly I was being accepted for what I was and not what people thought I should be. I left Belfast with more peace of mind than I was used to experiencing in my home town, and it was a feeling that would thankfully remain with me.

Kenneth Branagh – local boy made good; Belfast audiences were 'just plain delighted' to see him when his Renaissance Theatre Company came to the Grand Opera House in the summer of 1988.
PACEMAKER PRESS INTERNATIONAL

In 1990 Branagh returned with Renaissance to present the first performance of a new production of *Look Back in Anger*, and through his generosity the Ulster Youth Theatre benefited from the very good box office receipts. Eric Reid, the house manager, recalls that the set for this production was no more trouble-free than that for the previous occasion. At 7.20 p.m., with a full house waiting at the door, Kenneth Branagh was still striding around in the stalls, shouting 'I'm sorry, Eric, it's not right. I'm sorry, Eric, it has to be right.' It says much for both that Eric refers to Kenneth Branagh as 'good friend, nice guy'. A year later Renaissance brought *Uncle Vanya*, with Richard Briers and Peter Egan in the leading parts, and although they came again in the traditionally difficult period of June, they managed to revive a disappointing box office period with well-supported houses. In 1990 the Grand Opera House stage was filled by one of the largest casts ever assembled for local playwright Martin Lynch's community play *The Stone Chair*, a moving picture of life in Belfast in the Second World War, which was enthusiastically received.

Michael Barnes continued to take risks with the shows he brought. There were disappointments and some of the finest productions were poorly supported. Even big names such as Derek Jacobi and Colin Blakely did not bring in audiences for subjects not immediately appealing to Belfast. Only 32 per cent audiences saw the unique Philippe Genty Company perform *Forget-Me-Not*. Those who did describe it as one of the most memorable shows they have seen at the Grand Opera House.

The period of early summer has always been difficult to fill and only a sure crowd-puller like Kenneth Branagh could guarantee good houses. And the Belfast public could prove to be irritatingly fickle in its response to chosen programmes.

As predicted, the finances of the Grand Opera House were always precarious. By the end of its first full year after reopening, the theatre had attracted average houses of 77 per cent, a figure that most theatres would be proud to publish, and throughout the 1980s the Grand Opera House was able to maintain that proportion of tickets sold. In a good year the box office receipts would cover the costs of the productions, leaving the house costs of around £380,000 to be covered by Arts Council grant. By the end of the decade, however, the theatre had managed to turn a regular deficit into a surplus. The overall income was in excess of one million pounds and the theatre was high on the table of touring theatres in terms of both percentage houses and gross takings. Arts Council funding had been increased and the Grand Opera House benefited from this. In addition, the management was beginning to take advantage of the revenue available through sponsorship.

Frank Finlay appeared with Toyah Wilcox in *Peter Pan* at the Grand Opera House in 1995.
DAVID GRAHAM OF HILLSBOROUGH

It was a time of buoyancy, a buoyancy that was reflected to a remarkable degree in the streets of Belfast. From the darkened, sinister, empty urban landscape of the 1970s, the city had turned round to become a defiantly lively place at night, despite the continuing campaigns of bombing and murder. Restaurants of real quality sprang up, pubs that had closed at 8 or 9 p.m. were bursting at the doors at 11. Clubs throbbed with music or alternative comedy. The best rock bands came back. Big-name fast food chains set up restaurants close to the city centre. The area from Great Victoria Street to Queen's University became known as 'the golden mile', and it was widely acknowledged that the 'act of faith' that had been the reopening of the Grand Opera House had been the catalyst for this regeneration.

Few publications of the Northern Ireland Tourist Board, which had also been a prime mover in the restoration of the theatre, did not include a picture of a packed, sumptuous theatre, filled with relaxed and sophisticated patrons. It was exactly the image that many wished to portray of the battered city. The historian Jonathan Bardon, writing in 1982, puts the theatre's restoration into a contemporary perspective:

Rula Lenska performed in *Dangerous Corner* at the Grand Opera House in 1995.
DAVID GRAHAM OF HILLSBOROUGH

The interior of the Grand Opera House suffered severe damage after the May 1993 bomb.
BELFAST TELEGRAPH

For many the refurbishing of the Grand Opera House and its reopening . . . in the autumn of 1980, was the most striking and visible sign of the city's refusal to die.

The Grand Opera House could not have been restored by local funds alone. By 1982 Belfast had become a city ever more dependent on a kind of drip-feed from Westminster. Damaged as the city is by indigenous violence, world-wide recession and the austere economic policy of central government, it is still a living entity with the power of growth and renewal. Throughout its turbulent history it has shown a capacity for stoic endurance, adaptation and creativity.

The contrast between the Belfast of 1990 and the Belfast of 1980 is vividly highlighted by the theatre's technical manager, John Jordan. The Friday before the 1980 reopening night, he was having a drink in the nearby Crown Liquor Saloon. There was just himself and Sammy, the newspaper seller, in the bar, and as was customary the manager closed the pub at 9.00 p.m. John Jordan went out and walked up the white line in the middle of Great Victoria Street. The only sign of life in the desolate streetscape was a light and an open door at Ringo's fish-and-chip shop.

Having survived the worst of the 1980s, however, the Grand Opera House ran into turbulence of the most drastic kind when it suffered two massive bombs in the early 1990s. In December 1991 and May 1993, the theatre was severely damaged. The first of the bombs deprived the centre of Belfast of its premier pantomime, but the theatre was reopened in nine months. The May 1993 bomb came in the middle of the Ulster Amateur Drama Finals. With the staff again working to a very tight schedule, with a determination to lose as little time as possible, the theatre, which was more badly affected by the second blast, was able to mount a pantomime seven months later, although the closure meant that many members of staff decided to accept redundancy and Opera Northern Ireland lost its season for the second time.

But for the second time the Grand Opera House bounced back, picking up where it left off and getting ready to play host to one of the most momentous nights of its history, when the BAFTA award ceremony, with many of the theatre world's leading luminaries, led by Lord Attenborough, came to Belfast, in September 1994. Within months, on 17 March, St Patrick's Day, 1995, the theatre reached another landmark when the first segment of BBC's Comic Relief fund-raising marathon to come from outside London was broadcast from the stage of the Grand Opera House. Lenny Henry made an express journey from London to Belfast to finish the show here in the company of Julian Clary, Jo Brand and Patrick Kielty, a young local comedian, who was generally acknowledged to have stolen the show from his more experienced colleagues.

The bomb in May 1993 tore the side out of the building, but the Grand Opera House was able to stage a pantomime only seven months later.
BELFAST TELEGRAPH

It was a momentous period in other ways. It was decided that the Grand Opera House would operate more efficiently and creatively independent of direct Arts Council control and funding, and the theatre was leased to a board of trustees in April 1994 under the chairmanship of George Priestley OBE. The existing committee of the Grand Opera House, which was made up of Brian Baird, chairman of the Association of Business Sponsorship of the Arts, Phillip Price of Coopers & Lybrand, Cecil Ward, chairman of the Ulster Orchestra, Roy Johnston, music historian and former chairman of the Music and Opera Committee of the Arts Council of Northern Ireland, and Professor Colin Radford, former chairman of the Arts Council of Northern Ireland, was augmented by new members Jackie D'Arcy, director of communications at the Northern Ireland Tourist Board, Eleanor Methven of Charabanc Theatre Company, Catherine Toner of Northern Ireland Market Surveys, and James Hunt of Burns & Hunt Accountants. This new board of trustees would now hold responsibility for the management, direction and financial control of the theatre. George Priestley was confident that the board had the expertise to overcome the changing conditions which the theatre had to meet:

Milo O'Shea (left) and Lord Attenborough pictured together at the BAFTA awards ceremony at the Grand Opera House in September 1994
PACEMAKER PRESS INTERNATIONAL

> The new appointments now mean that the Grand Opera House has a unique blend of experienced professionals, representing Commerce and Industry, the Arts and Private and Public Sectors. It is a truly exciting time for the Grand

17 March 1995: part of BBC's Comic Relief programme is broadcast live from the Grand Opera House stage.
PACEMAKER PRESS INTERNATIONAL

Opera House and with the continuing support of the Northern Ireland public and the Arts Council, we look forward to an even brighter future.

An era came to an end in 1994 when Michael Barnes, who had done so much to endear the theatre to the Belfast public, and to woo reluctant artistes to its boards, decided to retire. His contribution was marked by a large photograph in the gallery bar, and by the naming of the circle bar MJB.

His place was taken by Derek Nicholls, a name and a face new to Northern Ireland but a theatre director and administrator of long experience, who had held posts as artistic director of the Theatre Royal in York and as director of the Midlands Arts Centre in Birmingham, where he had developed a particular interest in linking the work of professional artistes and companies with education and community projects. His initial aim was to ensure that there would be plenty for all on the stage at the Grand Opera House at affordable prices and that visiting theatre should become a quality experience in every respect. He quickly assessed the challenges and the advantages of the Grand Opera House as a theatre, recognising the unquantifiable asset of the affection and respect in which the theatre is held by the people of the city, and ambitious to make it a vibrant and useful part of the life of the wider community.

Throughout the period following the reopening in 1980 the theatre had become a vital part of Belfast life. It had proved itself readily adaptable to many forms of art. Those who played in it, managed it and attended it were struck by the way in which the Grand Opera House could 'expand or contract' according to the show being presented, whether it was a major drama, a ballet, or a country-and-western concert. It could be grand for the grand occasion or intimate for the one-man show, and the relationship between auditorium and stage demonstrated that Matcham's genius could serve the productions of the twentieth century as well as it did the productions of the nineteenth.

One of the best assessments of the Grand Opera House comes from Hilary Finch, opera critic of *The Times*, who has come to Belfast often through its recent history:

Frank Matcham's Grand Opera House is for me a beacon of Belfast. Its balance of the decorative, the eccentric and the celebratory in its architecture,

Derek Nicholls, appointed theatre director of the Grand Opera House in June 1994
GRAND OPERA HOUSE

of the monumental and the intimate, have a unique effect on the human spirit. Even in the most tense of recent times, one steps inside to an atmosphere of relaxed, yet excited audience expectation. I look forward to every return visit.

The Royal Flanders Ballet production of *La Sylphide* at the Grand Opera House in November 1990
CHRISTOPHER HILL PHOTOGRAPHIC

"CHARLES OF THE CITY."

(Mr. C. J. Brennan, Mus. B., F.R.C.O., City Organist and Conductor of City Amateur
Operatic Society, &c., &c.)

Madame Gertrude Drinkwater was the leading figure in the Ulster Operatic Company from her days as prima donna in 1909 until her retirement in 1946, which was marked by a presentation by the prime minister of Northern Ireland, Sir Basil Brooke.
GRAND OPERA HOUSE

10

THE AMATEUR MOVEMENT

AS EARLY AS 1896, the amateurs of Belfast society were welcomed on to the stage of the Grand Opera House, a tradition which has been continued ever since. When the Belfast Operatic Society presented *Paul Jones* before an appreciative and well-filled house that year they were not only the first amateurs to appear in the theatre but also the first company to sing any opera there. The critic of the *Belfast News-Letter* was impressed and encouraging:

We think that the members of this society have every reason to feel gratified with the progress they have made, and if they work with the same zeal as they have hitherto been doing, and are resolved to rest content with nothing less than a high measure of excellence, a bright and useful future should be before them. We have not listened with greater gratification to an amateur performance of the kind. We continually hear it said that allowance must be made for those who do not claim to be of the professional rank. This is only just, but, at the same time, as we have remarked, the amateurs of a bygone age would not be tolerated now at all. There is often very little difference between amateur and professional artists, one branch proves frequently to be a stepping stone to the other. But, judging by what we heard last night, the

Opposite:
Charles Brennan, city organist and conductor of the City Amateur Operatic Society, was a major influence in Belfast's musical circles throughout the first half of the century.
NOMAD

members of the Belfast Operatic Society have no reason to make the stereo-typed plea. As the evening progressed many of those present must have forgotten altogether that they were listening to amateurs.

That the Wardens father and son were willing to give a place to the amateur movement was generous but unsurprising. The first venture into the flourishing ranks of the operatic societies proved successful in filling houses, but the family seem also to have been very positive in their encouragement and help. Fred Warden had handled the stage management for the Ulster Amateur Operatic Society when, having been established for only two years, they took the big step from concert presentations in the Ulster Hall to the Theatre Royal to present a fairly ambitious, if predictable programme of *Maritana*, *Cavalleria rusticana* and *Faust*, and in the same way as their rivals in the Belfast Operatic Society, they had achieved commendable critiques and healthy houses.

The Grand Opera House continued to host the amateur operatic singers from these early days, and a significant production took place in April 1909, when it was announced:

All arrangements are now definitely settled in connection with the forthcoming amateur opera season at the Opera House during the week commencing 19th inst. Both phases of opera – classic and light – will be presented. Cavalleria Rusticana and I Pagliacci will be presented on all nights with the joyous San Toy. It is something that the City Amateur Opera Society is able from its membership to present two separate casts. So while Madame Drinkwater will be the prima donna in the classic operas, Miss Florence Macnaughten with Miss Elsie Parrot as understudy, will play the title role in San Toy. Mr C. J. Brennan has been unsparing in conducting his forces – both vocal and instrumental – to perfection.

Members of the cast of *San Toy*, produced by the City Amateur Operatic Society in 1909.

PUBLIC RECORD OFFICE OF NORTHERN IRELAND

The combination of two powerful personalities and dedicated musicians, Madame Drinkwater and Charles Brennan, would have a significant influence on the development of music in the city.

Madame Drinkwater led the Ulster Amateur Operatic Company for many years. She was a charismatic figure, originally from Wales, who had been trained as a singer by Ivor Novello's mother, Clara Novello Davies, and had won every possible prize at the national eisteddfods. She had twice toured the United States with Madame Davies, had won the Soprano Prize at the Chicago World Fair, and had sung before Queen Victoria at Osborne. She is still remembered with great affection and respect by her pupils and the singers of the company. Married to an army officer, Colonel Robert Hill, she lived an erratic life in a big rambling house near Carrickfergus. Her dedication to music was absolute, and she commanded her forces with energy and style. When conducting, Madame Drinkwater would always wear a hat for matinées and a full-length black or wine-coloured dress with lace for evening performances, with white gloves and her hair in a comb. She had also a great sense of humour and was highly entertaining.

A tiny figure 'about the height of two turf' as one friend described her, she was once working with Sir Tyrone Guthrie, who was well over six feet tall. An artistic crisis had been resolved and a friend remarked that she could now lay her head on Guthrie's shoulder and relax. 'If I laid it anywhere,' she said, 'it would have to be on his hip.' She was described as a 'diminutive and brightly coloured object, moving swiftly through Wellington Place', where she had her studio, above Hart & Churchill. She continued to teach throughout the worst of the Second World War, taking classes in the evening, despite the blitz. Claude Douglas and Harry Auld, leading figures in the company, recalled how she would complete the class with the injunction, 'Wrap up well, dear boy', and set off to the bus station in Smithfield, with her torch, through the blackout. Claude Douglas, her pupil, tried to accompany her whenever possible, because she had been knocked down once. He remembers how, once she reached and boarded the bus, she would insist on sitting in the front seat if she could get it and use the torch out of the window to guide the bus northwards from Belfast, much to the irritation of the bus drivers. As she continued with her career as supremo of the company, stories of her eccentricities developed. One performance went awry as Madame energetically swatted a fly away with her baton, and on another occasion a musician was convinced that she was reading the score upside down.

There was no doubt, however, that the success of the company owes an enormous debt to this extraordinary woman. In a programme of 1939, she provided an overview of the company's work:

> The Ulster Amateur Operatic Company originated from a Recital of Operatic Arias and Scenas given by my pupils in a small hall in the year 1910.
>
> In successive years, performances of a more ambitious character such as 'Midsummer Night's Dream', 'Sleeping Beauty', 'Persian Princess', 'Iolanthe' (girls' chorus only), Scenes from 'Faust', 'Il Trovatore', and 'Hansel and Gretel' were undertaken.
>
> The introduction of men into the Company made possible the production of full opera, and the first of these was given in 1918 in the Grand Opera House – the 'Gondoliers' and 'Iolanthe' being performed. Since then the 'Opera Week' has become an annual event, and the following is a list of the operas given by the Company.
>
> 'Iolanthe' (4 times), 'Gondoliers' (4 times), 'Mikado' (twice), 'Trial by Jury' (3 times), 'Yeomen of the Guard', 'Princess Ida', 'Pirates of Penzance', 'Dido and Aeneas', 'Rose of Auvergne', 'Merrie England', 'La Fille de Madame Angot', 'Love in a Village', 'Maid of the Mountains', 'Desert Song', 'Rose Marie', 'New Moon', 'No, No, Nanette'.

The standard of the Ulster Operatic Company's marketing and public relations was extremely high. Most productions throughout the 1940s and 1950s were accompanied by sophisticated hand bills and programmes.
BOB McKEOWN

Such was the regard in which she was held that when she retired in 1946, the public presentation to Madame Gertrude Drinkwater, MBE, LRAM, was made by the prime minister of Northern Ireland, the Right Honourable Sir Basil Brooke, and the occasion was chaired by Major J. Maynard Sinclair, the Minister of Finance.

In the period before and after the Second World War, the level of the company's productions grew very sophisticated. Often the company would hire a production of a popular operetta, straight from a run in London. The costumes were first-rate too. Harry Auld remembers being given a cloak

from the wardrobe department with the name of the celebrated actor Matheson Lang sewn into the lining. The company imported first-class producers, and it was one of these, Jack Stock, who had been coming to Belfast for several years, who in 1944 hinted that perhaps the administration could be just a little better organised. He suggested to Harry Auld that members might persuade Madame to form a company, with a committee. The first reaction was that Madame would never agree to that, but she did, and Harry held a meeting in the office of his shop, Auld & Pemberton, Tobacconists, in Donegall Place. He asked Harold Taggart to become the

The Ulster Operatic Company's production of *The Yeomen of the Guard* in 1948, with Betty Norman, Claude Douglas and Denis Suffern
CLAUDE DOUGLAS

Marjorie McKee and Claude Douglas
in the Ulster Operatic Society's
production of *No, No, Nanette*
in 1936
CLAUDE DOUGLAS

chairman and put the company on a proper footing.

One of the great strengths of the amateur operatic tradition was the Ladies' Committee, which not only raised money for charity but used its considerable influence to encourage patronage. After the 1909 production of the City Amateur Operatic Society, £390 was handed over to the National Society for the Prevention of Cruelty to Children, Nazareth Lodge, the Samaritan Hospital and the Ulster Hospital for Sick Children. The Ulster Amateur Operatic Company had an enviable list of energetic and influential society ladies to help. The Duchess of Abercorn was president, and the leader of London society, Lady Londonderry, was involved in several fund-raising operas. Charitable causes helped by Opera Weeks included the Royal Red Cross, many of Belfast's hospitals and Dr Barnardo's. A favourite fund was the Shipwrecked Mariners' Society. In the three years before Madame Drinkwater's retirement in 1946, Opera Weeks raised over £6,000. The involvement of people of prestige lent glamour to the events and on the first Monday (now such a difficult night for any theatre to sell tickets for) the audience came in evening dress and there was a guest of honour, usually the Governor of Northern Ireland. Friday night was another dress night. These are remembered as great social occasions, and Madame Drinkwater herself was extremely popular with these important patrons.

Some ladies also helped behind stage, making tea for the cast in the interval, and during one celebrated performance one of these ladies, in a hat (they always wore a hat) and a cardigan (they always wore a cardigan), walked across the stage carrying two kettles, while Lady Turner's daughter was attempting to sing a solo.

Music rehearsals took place in Hart & Churchill, but stage rehearsals were held in a variety of rooms, including the Grand Central Hotel and a warehouse at the corner of Ormeau Avenue and Adelaide Street, where access was solely by means of a goods hoist. The company also used an extremely precarious building at the corner of High Street and Victoria Street. The rehearsal rooms were on the third floor at the top of a rickety wooden staircase, crammed with props and sets, above the premises of a tailor called Little. One night an apprentice tailor left an iron burning, and the company smelt the ominous whiff of smoke. The fire brigade was called and the singers were evacuated, but they counted themselves very fortunate to have escaped. These Victoria Street premises were also the venue for the last-night parties, and when the Rathmines and Rathgar Company came from Dublin to watch the shows, as they did regularly, they added greatly to the fun afterwards.

The rehearsal period would last several months, after which the singers were finally allowed into the Grand Opera House on the Saturday afternoon before the run began for the band call. The aim of this was to ensure harmony with the orchestra, which was made up of local professional musicians. Then on Sunday there was a full dress rehearsal with the entire company and the orchestra. This would begin at 11.00 a.m. and last until well into the night. On Monday the company would begin its two-week run. They could guarantee good houses throughout.

Backstage the amateur singers received exactly the same treatment as the stars who might have used the theatre the week before. Principal singers were granted the first dressing rooms, and they got their calls over the tannoy, their five-minute call and their flowers and telegrams at the stage door. The committee decided, however, that principals should not receive flowers on stage, as this took away from the important work achieved by the valuable members of the chorus. A Mr Doherty, a hairdresser in Great Victoria Street who sold theatrical make-up, would come along to make up the principals, and a member of the Ulster Operatic Company, Sybil Evans, the honorary patron's secretary, who was wonderful at make-up, would look after most of the chorus. When it came to the wardrobe, however, it was up to each individual player to be responsible for his or her costume, and on the last night it was a strict rule that each singer should ensure that every item of his or her costume should be tied together ready for the big skips to take them back to London or Manchester or Liverpool. Theatrical costumes were much too expensive for carelessness. The company regularly mounted matinée as well as evening performances, and Thompson's Restaurant was favoured as a place for the cast to refresh themselves before returning to the theatre.

The standard of the singing was extremely high, and in the programme of 1939 Madame Drinkwater proudly lists a roll of former members of the company 'who have since achieved prominence in the professional world'. Madame Minnie Hampton and Winifred Brady became prima donnas at the Old Vic and Sadler's Wells, three others went on to join Carl Rosa, several became scholars at the great music colleges and academies (three won scholarships in the same year) and others became well known as radio voices. Before the war, James Johnston sang in *The Desert Song* to George Allport's lead as the Red Shadow: 'only one solo, but it was beautiful', according to Claude Douglas. Douglas was for many years the principal man, with a very fine voice and an excellent stage presence. And in contrast to the amateur companies of today, who tend to have individual microphones, the singers on the stage before the 1960s were largely dependent on their own vocal power and the kind acoustics of the Grand Opera House. Professional opera still refuses to use any electronic aids, but then professional singers would never sing every night for two weeks, as the principals of amateur operatic companies did.

There was a distinguished group of singing teachers at this period working in Belfast and bringing forward new young voices. In addition to Madame Drinkwater, John Vine was an inspiring musician who took pupils in his studio on the Ravenhill Road, conducted the Harland & Wolff Male Voice Choir, and was the person who introduced James Johnston to Tyrone Guthrie. Captain Brennan, for many years the organist at St Anne's Cathedral and a monumental figure in Belfast's musical history, taught singers in Upper Crescent. Carys Davies taught at Belgravia at the time, and was much appreciated. The voice teacher Bertie Scott, who moved to London to work with many of the best actors and singers there, had also trained and given his advice to many young singers.

During the Second World War, when the Savoy Players were in residence in the Grand Opera House, the company moved to the Empire Theatre, but they soon returned to Great Victoria Street with the quality of productions and support undiminished. David Leinster had taken over the mantle of musical director from Madame Drinkwater, and his exacting standards ensured that the quality of the company remained high. Notable members of the company, under Harold Taggart as chairman, included Denis Suffern, Robert McKeown, Joseph Morrison, Owen Peacock, Richard Evans, Daphne Brittain, Marjorie McKee, Betty Shaw, Betty Norman and Ruth Johnston, with Harry Auld frequently featuring as producer. Denis Suffern was for a long period the leading man. A fine musician and actor, and genial and entertaining off stage, he had been asked to join D'Oyly Carte, but had decided to remain in the amateur ranks and in Northern Ireland. His experience and expertise was much in demand from younger operatic societies starting out. Later Desmond Anderson, David Black, Maureen Ashe and June Boyle made an outstanding contribution to the company.

Harry Auld was influential in persuading Madame Drinkwater to form the Ulster Operatic Company after the Second World War. Meetings were held in his tobacconists, Auld & Pemberton, Donegall Place.
BOB McKEOWN

The company enjoyed one of its most celebrated occasions in 1958, when Princess Margaret attended a gala performance of *Brigadoon* in aid of the National Society for the Prevention of Cruelty to Children. The production contained much that was best about the Ulster Operatic Company, as it was then known, and featured many of the names associated with the productions of the time. Denis Suffern, Robert McKeown, Desmond Anderson, David Erwin, Maureen Ashe and Betty Norman were among the singers presented to the princess. Also presented were Richard Evans, chairman of the company, David Leinster, musical director, Maxine Graham, dancing mistress, and Leslie Jones, producer. The programme, which was generously supported by advertisers, contained long lists of patrons, who each contributed two guineas. The production was enhanced by the contribution of the full-blooded sound of the Saintfield Pipe Band, under Pipe Major Joseph Gilmore. A full tide of success was running for the company, which approached all aspects of sponsorship and marketing in a very businesslike way. Under the heading 'Company Notes', the committee wrote thus:

> The Company is again very grateful for the support afforded to them by Messrs Inglis & Co. Ltd. who undertook to sponsor this production. Our relationship during *White Horse Inn* was a very happy one which we hope will continue for many years to come.
>
> When writing these notes the financial success of the Gala Evening of *Brigadoon* is assured and it gives us great pleasure to assist once again the National Society for the Prevention of Cruelty to Children.
>
> Again we have the support of many organised parties from country districts and within the city. We wish you all a very happy evening.

Eventually a combination of circumstances, finance and security, forced the company to leave the Grand Opera House and find new quarters in the Harberton Theatre in the Royal Ulster Agricultural Society's grounds at

The death scene from *Bitter Sweet*, performed by the Ulster Operatic Society at the Grand Opera House in 1949

CLAUDE DOUGLAS

The Ulster Operatic Company's
production of *Lilac Time* in 1956,
with Betty Norman, Bob McKeown,
Denis Suffern and Marjorie McKee
BOB McKEOWN

Balmoral. But the amateur operatic tradition continued at the Grand Opera House with regular seasons by other local societies, notably St Agnes's Choral Society, who have brought productions of a very high standard to the theatre, from *The King and I* in 1983 to *My Fair Lady* in 1995. From an early stage, the spread of audience that a local society like St Agnes's brought to the Grand Opera House had a discernible benefit in proving that the theatre could be an inviting place to go, and the platform that St Agnes's and other operatic societies were able to give to promising young singers such as Kate McCarney was invaluable.

In the Grand Opera House's first year of operation after reopening in 1980, the Association of Irish Music Societies (Northern Region) made a very special contribution, with *Cavalcade of Song – Tribute to the Grand Opera House and Cirque*. In this popular programme, members from nine societies, under musical director Billy Cairns, gave a selection of songs rich in nostalgia from the great musicals and operettas of the theatre's history: *Irene*, *The White Horse Inn*, *Lilac Time*, *Maritana*, *The Merry Widow*, together with a variety of music from Rodgers and Hammerstein and Gilbert and Sullivan. The evening, which closed with a dramatic finale in which the entire company sang the Chorus of the Hebrew Slaves, was expertly introduced by two personalities who had risen from the ranks of the amateur

movement, Gloria Hunniford and Gerry Kelly.

Although amateur drama was slower than amateur opera to come to the stage of the Grand Opera House, it played an equally important part in the history of the theatre and the cultural life of Northern Ireland. By the end of the 1920s the *feis*, which brought together the best amateur players to the finals in the Grand Opera House, was an annual event. In 1936 the *feis* organised by the Northern Drama League, which was adjudicated by Lennox Robinson, included the Bangor Unemployed Men, the Irish Bank Officials, and the Enniskillen Amateur Dramatic Society produced by Marie Trimble.

This period witnessed a great boom in amateur dramatic societies, and it became obvious that the existing umbrella organisation, the British Drama League, was now unable to cover the needs of the expanding movement and that there was a need for some co-ordination of the activities of the various groups, specifically in Northern Ireland. Attempts to form such a body were made by organisations including the Association of Ulster Amateur Dramatic Societies and the Ulster Drama League, which unfortunately found themselves covering the same ground. The Association of Ulster Amateur Dramatic Societies, led by men such as Sidney Hewitt, Eddie Fullalove, Paddy Bogues and Frank Reynolds, who later became the

Bob McKeown and Betty Shaw in *The Student Prince,* performed in the Grand Opera House in 1952
BETTY McILWAINE

manager of the Empire, had achieved considerable success, but had been badly hit by debts from the association's magazine *Script*.

By 1949, the amateur drama festival movement was particularly strong, and the desirability of an organising body had become an urgent need, and so the Association of Ulster Drama Festivals (AUDF) came into being, largely on the initiative of James Henry Cathcart of Larne Drama Festival, who became the first chairman with the support and assistance of members of the Ballymoney and Newry festivals. As the governing body of drama festival activity in the province, the aims of the AUDF are to 'foster and encourage amateur drama through the holding of Festivals of Drama, the promotion and co-operation between Ulster Drama Festivals, and the fostering of relations with cognate and similar organisations in Northern Ireland and other regions'. The association is the body responsible for the complicated but effective judging process that brought the best of amateur talent to the Grand Opera House for many years. Unfortunately, though, despite the repeatedly stated aim of co-ordinating activities, the association, throughout its forty-five years of history, has never quite been able to avoid clashes of dates.

In 1951, as part of the Festival of Britain, a very successful drama festival was organised in Bangor, under the auspices of the Council for the Encouragement of Music and the Arts, by Sidney Hewitt: in 1953 Ted Phillipson and James Henry Cathcart made an exploratory approach to George Lodge of the Grand Opera House to explore whether the finals might be held at the theatre. Lodge agreed, and that began a run of Grand Opera House finals until the temporary decline of the theatre and the Troubles nineteen years later forced the drama finals out, first to the Little Theatre, Bangor, and then to the Chichester Theatre in the County Hall, Ballymena. In 1980, the finals returned to the Grand Opera House, where they remained until 1995, when it was decided that a move to the smaller Lyric Theatre would be more economical and might resolve the problem of very poor houses on certain nights of the week.

During finals week in the Grand Opera House the festival enjoyed the regular patronage of successive governors of Northern Ireland and lord mayors of Belfast, and accumulated an impressive array of trophies for competition. George Lodge presented the Grand Opera House Challenge Cup for the best production. Rowel Friers, the cartoonist and association vice-president, gave a trophy for decor, the Arts and Group theatres gave awards for best actor and actress, and the *News Letter* trophy went to the best producer. Adjudicators of the highest calibre have been persuaded to come to the Grand Opera House finals. Tyrone Guthrie and Ray McAnally were two outstanding and stimulating adjudicators, Ronald Mason, Head of BBC Radio Drama, came back to his roots to judge, and Hilton Edwards was memorable in this capacity: very much the actor, grand and theatrical but sound.

Those plays that reached finals had gone through a challenging process of elimination and played in spaces very different to that of the Grand

Opera House stage. Everyone has their favourite memory, from the huge thousand-seater parochial hall in Carrickmore, which is filled regularly, to the very fine suppers produced by Eve Reynolds at Bangor, to the problems of struggling up an outside metal staircase with sets and props at Ballymoney and, way back in the distant memory, the transport by cattle truck of the Aughnacloy Players to Enniskillen.

The festival was very fortunate to have as president for many years Angela, Countess of Antrim. From her home at Glenarm Castle she was associated with Larne Dramatic Society. A gifted artist, as president she was no mere figurehead but took a very active interest in the development of the festival and the work of the committee. Her position as chairwoman of Ulster Television afforded to the festival one very special privilege. For a wonderful period of time, finals-night parties were held in the studios of Ulster Television. These were great parties, with a magnificent atmosphere; tickets for admission were at a premium, and Lady Antrim would arrive burdened with bottles of champagne for the winners. This handsome tradition continued when Brum Henderson CBE, of Ulster Television took over the president's position, but eventually, and quite reasonably, the television company felt that the dust created by the event was too damaging for the extremely sensitive equipment in the studios and the finals-night party moved to the Plaza Hotel.

Alan Reynolds, a vice-president of the society, is in no doubt about the achievements of the AUDF. He feels that the festivals and the much-coveted places in the finals are the best incentive for raising and maintaining standards. The competitive system offers a goal for societies, and a progression among friendly rivalry which is only productive. It leads to a climate of operation in which great attention to detail is essential. And every amateur dramatic company loves to come to a professional theatre, to work with professional theatre staff, and to play on a great stage, with wonderful acoustics and a full auditorium. Every amateur seems to have nothing but praise for the Grand Opera House staff, and the reception that is given to each company. Particularly deserving of praise for his co-operation is the current technical manager, John Jordan, who got used to all the companies' self-confessed idiosyncrasies, and who was a special favourite for his comic remarks and wry faces on the nights of the presentation. One amateur actress remembers a day at the Grand Opera House when, wanting to savour every minute of her time there, she arrived early, got everything done and, finding the stage and the auditorium deserted, the safety curtain raised, she thought she might use this delicious moment to say a few of her lines to the house. Her voice rang out, she relished the fine acoustics, she took a breath to start again, and a loud caustic drawl emerged from the wings. 'Bloody Glenda Jackson.' It was John Jordan.

For the technical staff of the theatre, it was an extraordinary period. Accustomed to getting a show in and out each week, they had to adapt to a different play, a different set, and a different lighting scheme each night, sometimes working with backstage crews who had never been in the theatre before. Occasionally producers took the opportunity to experiment with the extra facilities the Grand Opera House could offer a small company, as Alan Reynolds did for *The Love of Four Colonels*. He speaks of the feeling of intense excitement standing alone way, way up in the dark, at the top of the fly tower, with the theatre still rising high above him, with a huge piece of gauze he had introduced as a special effect, with the stage 'miles below', waiting for the signal to lower it from the fly. The problem of adapting a production to fit the wide spaces of the Grand Opera House stage sometimes tempted amateur producers to widen and stretch out the set. Beth Duffin, the honorary secretary of the AUDF, who has seen many productions and produced prize-winning plays herself, believes this is a mistake. She has every faith in the famous capacity of the Grand Opera House to adapt to the compact just as it adapts to the massive in scale.

John Knipe MBE, an AUDF vice-president, will claim another major achievement for the society. Because Northern Ireland has never had a theatre school, the amateur dramatic societies are in many ways the prime educators of any artistic talent which may be latent in the community. The list of former society members, of actors and actresses who have played their parts in the festivals and often in the finals, and then gone on to become well known in the British theatre or the world of entertainment, certainly bears this out. Doreen Hepburn and Colin Blakely started in Bangor; Derek Bailey, television and film director, and Anne Gregg, television personality, were in the Belfast Drama Circle; Ronald Mason, Head of BBC Radio Drama for the UK, began in Coleraine; Denys Hawthorne and James Greene were in Queen's University, Belfast, Dramsoc; Oscar nominee Liam Neeson started out in the Slemish Players in Ballymena; Ciaran Hinds was a member of the Clarence Players in Belfast. In addition the list of amateurs turned professional who have made a significant contribution to the cultural life of the province is a long one – including people like Linda Wray, Walter Love, Trudy Kelly, J.J. Murphy, Sam Thompson, Rowel Friers, Helen Madden, Liam O'Callaghan, Michael Duffy and Sam Macready.

Liam Neeson's rise from being John, the Witch Boy, in the Slemish Players' *Dark of the Moon* in 1973 to his portrayal of Schindler in the film *Schindler's List* is a progression of which the amateur movement is very proud. It was also intensely proud of Colin Blakely. Phyllis Knipe of Bangor is given credit for spotting this remarkable talent when he was

Many Happy Returns

Ken, Austin, Gerda Redlich, Doreen Hepburn, Linda Wray, Liam O'Callaghan, Rowel Friers, Leslie Stuart, Helen Madden (Miss Helen)
Sybil Allen   Walter Love   George O'Prey   Olivia Nash
Trudy Kelly   Ronald Mason   Colin Blakely.

The cartoonist Rowel Friers is a vice-president of the Association of Ulster Drama Festivals, and he regularly contributed to festival programmes. The 1973 programme included many members who went on to become professionals in the world of theatre and broadcasting.
ALAN REYNOLDS

playing Poor Judd in Bangor Operatic's production of *Oklahoma!* She is quoted as identifying him as just the chap they needed, and she held onto him, and did not let go, until he had signed up. Colin Blakely had a secure future in the Belfast shop the Athletic Stores, which was the family business, but he opted for the stage. In 1973, when the festival had been forced out of the Grand Opera House by the Troubles but was celebrating its twenty-first birthday, he sent it his very good wishes:

> My congratulations on the Ulster Drama Festival's 'coming of age' in May. Although you have, sadly, been forced to abandon the Opera House, I am particularly pleased that your new home should be the Little Theatre in Bangor where I first tremblingly uttered on a stage.
>
> With the entire spectrum of theatre in Northern Ireland having suffered so much in the present troubled times, including the tragic loss of the Arts Theatre, the role of the Ulster Drama Festival is ever increasingly vital.
>
> So in addition to my thanks and admiration for all your achievements so far, to your flourishing future,
> My best wishes,
> Sincerely
> Colin Blakely

Sir Bernard Miles, administrator of the Mermaid Theatre and adjudicator in 1955, added his congratulations:

> I well remember my very happy visit. I congratulate you on having survived

Liam Neeson in the Field Day production of Brian Friel's *Translations* in 1980. Neeson is one of the many actors who made their way through the amateur ranks to the professional stage. In 1973 he appeared in the Slemish Players' *The Dark of the Moon.*
FIELD DAY

as an active artistic agent in the City of Belfast for twenty one years and wish you a successful journey on towards your century. By that time neither you or any present members will be on the muster roll but lending a moral and spiritual hand from the Great Beyond.

Warmest greetings to you all and Congratulations.

Bernard Miles.

Over the years the fortunes of individual societies have flourished or declined. Some societies that were pre-eminent in the early years, such as Instonians' Dramatic Society or Coleraine Drama Club, have folded and others have taken their place. The quality of the plays chosen continues to be universally high, however, and often Northern Ireland audiences were given the chance to see the works of playwrights that few local commercial theatres would risk because of the box office liability. At the same time amateur companies are naturally drawn to Irish writers, and often the list of finalists has been equally divided between plays with a local interest and challenging or esoteric choices. A list of festival finalists between 1953 and 1972 included plays by O'Casey, Synge, Shiels, Tomelty, Keane, Friel and Behan as well as Anouilh, Sophocles, O'Neill, Giraudoux, Chekhov, Miller, Fry, Brecht and Lorca. The record of ambition and achievement in choice of plays after 1980 is no less impressive, with the same adventurous mix of international and Irish writers, but this time as well as Anouilh, Tennessee Williams, Chekhov there were the works of contemporary Northern Irish writers Christina Reid, Martin Lynch and Graham Reid. In an extraordinary festival season, both Bangor and Newpoint presented Frank McGuinness's *Observe the Sons of Ulster Marching Towards the Somme*, and both productions were successful in reaching the finals. In a tense week, Newpoint Players under Sean Hollywood just came out top to win the challenge. Some companies have regularly opted for comedy. Bangor had a notable success with *Hay Fever*, but the general experience has been that the contemporary humour of Alan Ayckbourn or Neil Simon does not travel exceptionally well across either Irish Sea or Atlantic Ocean and that local companies do better with local laughter.

The choice of play has always been a difficult one for the local clubs and societies. Often the final decision rests with the person whose responsibility it will be to produce the work. Some societies have been able to follow the dictum that John Knipe quotes slightly ironically, that a director's first duty is to find a play with as big a cast as possible. Sean Hollywood, at Newpoint, has been outstandingly successful in this, and has been instrumental in enabling a large number of young people to experience drama at first hand. His production of *Under Milk Wood* in 1982 had sixty-seven parts. More usually a producer will tailor the choice of play to the talent available, and will occasionally pick a play specifically as a vehicle for a particularly talented actor or actress.

The problem of finding suitable works was especially difficult during the Second World War, but this was a problem that John Knipe overcame in an unusual way. Working as a customs officer, he was making his usual inspection of an American vessel when the conversation with its captain turned to matters theatrical. It soon became obvious that the captain was an enthusiast, and he spoke admiringly of a play he had very much enjoyed recently in New York. It was called *Our Town*, by Thornton Wilder. First presented in 1938, it is a touching look at small-town American life, had been presented experimentally using minimal props and sets, and had won the Pulitzer Prize for the year. The captain undertook to bring some scripts back with him on his next trip. He was as good as his word, and *Our Town*, fresh from New York, was duly performed by the Bangor Drama Club, its European première.

On only rare occasions have amateur drama companies decided to take on Shakespeare, but when they were brave enough to do so, it has often been remarkably successful. The Osborne Players reached the finals with both *Macbeth* and *Hamlet*, produced by Nevin Harris, with sets designed by Ulster artist Dick Croft. Plays from the classical British repertory, however, are not often performed. John Knipe tells the tale of the adjudication of Bangor Drama Club's production of *She Stoops to Conquer*. The adjudicator, while praising the excellence of the production, regretted that the classic costume dramas were not more often put on; it was, he supposed, just too expensive to costume these. John

May 1993: Irwin Murphy and Carole Stewart in the Holywood Players' *84, Charing Cross Road*. It was after this performance had ended and the stage had been cleared that a bomb exploded, causing severe damage to the Grand Opera House.
CAROLE STEWART

Knipe says that the Bangor cast and production team nodded sagely at these words, knowing in fact that the whole play had been dressed at a cost of about £2 4s. 3d. Phyllis Knipe was not only an expert needlewoman, but also possessed a great memory for costumes in past productions. When a costume was owned by someone else, she had a most persuasive line in borrowing, which began in extravagant praise for the dress, and ended in convincing the owner that really such a fine costume deserved to be seen again.

Within the great variety of plays the standards have been maintained to a very high level. Those who have watched decades of finals applaud the undeniable improvement in technical and staging expertise, but judge that the high standards of acting and production of the early days have not necessarily been surpassed.

The AUDF shot into unwelcome limelight in May 1993, when a bomb destroyed part of the Grand Opera House. It was right in the middle of finals week and the Holywood Players had just performed a wonderful production of *84, Charing Cross Road*, directed by Beth Duffin and with a captivating performance by Carole Stewart who remembers her feelings at the time:

> It was every amateur drama company's dream to reach the Ulster Finals at the Opera House. Holywood Players played on that night in May to the largest audience ever for an amateur company. *84, Charing Cross Road* had played to great success on the Festival circuit, but this was the highlight of the run in the province. Helene Hanff's last line

of the play is '. . . I finally made it.' The play went down to a great response and a warm adjudication from Barry Cassin. A long time was spent cleaning the stage, sweeping the floors, and leaving the gorgeous dressing rooms ready for the next company to come in the next morning – 'leave as you expect to find it' was the ringing order of the midnight call. It seemed unreal to waken to the horrific news that early next morning all that cleaning had been in vain. The Opera House was in rubble again.

It was a day of frantic activity, centred around honorary secretary Beth Duffin, members of the AUDF committee, Michael Barnes, general administrator and artistic director, and many well-wishers. Every possible alternative venue was explored and Beth Duffin declared that the show would go on, even if it was in a tent lit by hurricane lamps.

In the end, the hall at St Bartholomew's in Stranmillis Road was secured. St Bart's has been a happy home for local drama for many years, and the festival was assured of a warm and experienced welcome. The company to step into this vacuum was Theatre 3 Newtownabbey. Maureen Dunn, who was taking the part of Mrs Venable in *Suddenly Last Summer*, describes arriving at the hall, with their set, which had been all loaded up the night before, to find the church's pantomime set still in place. Permission was finally granted to dismantle the pantomime set, but the company's vision of a dramatic set of wonderful huge passionflowers, designed to look stunning against the black curtains and wide open spaces of the Grand Opera House, did not look quite the same in the church hall. And the bulky vintage wheelchair, which had been obtained with great difficulty, was almost impossible to manoeuvre on the smaller stage.

The spirit of co-operation, however, was inspiring. The Grand Opera House technical staff, under John Jordan, did everything they could to smoothe the way for the Newtownabbey company, and the front-of-house staff assisted in every way as well. Brum Henderson arrived to roll up his sleeves and put out chairs, and television crews and press people were everywhere. In fact, as Maureen Dunn was making her final preparation just before curtain-up, after a fraught day, the door was thrown open and a camera crew burst in. As the curtains opened she found herself staring straight into another lens.

Michael Barnes made a most moving speech, praising the dedication and lauding the determination and spirit of the amateurs. He was enormously proud of them. In the standing ovation that followed, there was hardly a dry eye in the house.

Grand Opera House, Belfast
❖❖❖❖
BOOK OF SONGS
OF "GRAND" ANNUAL CHRISTMAS PANTOMIME

ALADDIN

First Production:
MONDAY (Xmas Day), DEC. 25th, 1933   Price Fourpence

S. C. ALLEN AND COMPANY, LTD., BELFAST AND LONDON

From Victorian times until the 1930s pantomimes were accompanied by elaborate song books, giving the words of popular songs.
LINEN HALL LIBRARY

11
THE PANTOMIME: 'SPECTACULAR AND INGENUOUS'

AS WITH MANY OTHER THEATRES, the Grand Opera House has relied on the enduring success of the pantomime as a financial lifeline to sustain the viability of the house. It has always been, from the era of J.F. Warden to that of Derek Nicholls in the 1990s, the one show, almost without fail, that the theatre has mounted as an in-house production. The tradition has continued with only very minor interruptions from the opening production of the theatre, the pantomime *Blue Beard, or Is Marriage a Failure?*, to the present day. Only the Second World War, the change of management in 1960, a dalliance with the musical as an alternative, and the Troubles caused a break in the perpetuity of this much-loved form of entertainment. Almost without fail the self-appointed artistic hierarchy has disdained the pantomime as an art form, and without fail the Belfast public has endorsed it by its overwhelming support. The Grand Opera House is the ideal theatre for a pantomime: warm, intimate, magical, traditional.

The financial benefits of the pantomime have been recognised by theatre managers for a very long time. In Drury Lane in the 1720s the appearance of the greatest actors of the day, including

Empsie Bowman as Cinderella
in 1905, during the time when the
Grand Opera House was known as
the Palace of Varieties
GRAND OPERA HOUSE

Jenny Bonney as Princess Belle in the
1905 production of *Cinderella*
GRAND OPERA HOUSE

Colley Cibber and Mrs Oldfield, could expect to raise £500 a week, whilst a good season of pantomime would draw in £1,000 a week. William Charles Macready, the great tragedian, tells in his diaries of acute anxiety about an ill-prepared pantomime in the 1830s when he was manager of Covent Garden. He had to spend nine and a half hours on Christmas Eve whipping *Harlequin and Fair Rosamund*, or *Old Dame Nature and the Fairy Art*, into shape. He considered cancelling the show, which was beset by the inefficiency of the carpenters, but could not afford to waste the large capital investment. His worry caused him to give a poor performance in the forepiece, *Jane Shore*, and his fears were justified. The first night was a disaster. He wrote: 'What will be the result I cannot guess – it will go near to ruin me.' In the event the rest of the pantomime survived, the second night went smoothly, and financial disaster was averted. Even David Garrick set aside his personal preferences in the interests of financial pragmatism, to put on his first pantomime, 'An Entertainment with Italian Grotesque Characters' called *Queen Mab*, at Drury Lane in 1750. This production was an enormous success, and prompted Garrick to continue to present the genre in direct competition with Covent Garden.

The box office benefits that a pantomime brings to the finances of a theatre have resulted in some degree of enterprise by enthusiastic managers of the Grand Opera House. Several early pantomimes, including the very successful *Sleeping Beauty*, opened in Belfast and transferred to Dublin to perform equally well. In 1897 the *Belfast News-Letter* reported that *Dick Whittington* would run for five weeks from 24 December before transferring to Dublin, adding, 'It seems almost soft to wage that it will be a brilliant triumph in every way, despite the fact that Messrs Warden have selected the superstitious Friday for the embarkation of the momentous affair.'

Fred Warden optimistically attempted an occasional Easter pantomime, but these were not so popular as he might have hoped. Today, the management of the Grand Opera House would be severely disappointed if the Christmas pantomime did not attract houses of 85 per cent and receipts of over £500,000, testaments to a popularity that has continued for over two centuries.

One of the first recorded pantomimes, or ancestor of the pantomime, to be produced in Belfast was performed in the Vaults, Ann Street, on 3 January 1755, when *Harlequin Animated; or Fairy Friendship* was presented after *Conscious Lovers*. Four nights later *Hamlet* was given 'with a pantomime' in which 'will be introduced the surprising Escape of Harlequin into a Quart Bottle'. Very little of these early pantomimes bears much relationship to the spectacles of the Victorian stage or to the successfully formulaic productions of today. Continuing threads are the succession of stock characters: four lovers, including two gallants, caricatured old men, and a clownish maid. The Italian *commedia dell'arte* tradition, from which the harlequinade sprang, centred on improvisation of mime and dance, but was also heavily dependent on slapstick buffoonery, well-established, familiar character types, and well-known acts or turns similar in spirit to the circus clown or music-hall comedian, developed to become crucial to the performance.

In the nineteenth century, the harlequinade evolved in different ways, according to different nationalities and customs; the clown Grimaldi, the mime artist Marcel Marceau and Charlie Chaplin were all inheritors of the tradition. Once the Victorian pantomime was established, the pattern remained fairly constant, and from the first production of *Blue Beard* in the Grand Opera House the essentials of a good pantomime have changed very little, although even in 1895 the harlequinade had still survived in name at least, and was the last item in the programme of *Blue Beard*. A few years later, a Grand Opera House pantomime had a harlequinade at Scene 9, which had a clown, pantaloon, harlequina and columbine – and this was in a production that boasted wonderful electrical effects.

One of the successful elements of the pantomime is that it has been adept at embracing the most popular features of contemporary entertainment; through its history it has adopted as its own the clown, the 'breeches' roles, the music-hall song and community singing, and, most recently, the star of the television soap. Although pantomime has been very good at including these features, it has been very bad at letting them go, and that is one reason why so many pantomimes are well over three hours long. One material difference between the Victorian show and that of today is the introduction of the professional comic, which was a later feature, and one of which the Belfast management took full advantage.

So far as comedy was concerned, in the early years of the Grand Opera House it was vital that Victorian prudishness should not be offended by the pantomime productions. Mr Frederick Mouillot, who was responsible for many productions, insisted that the *Babes in the Wood* of 1898 would be 'a very fine pantomime in every sense', stressing that vulgarity on the stage was most objectionable and did the theatre a lot of harm. He added:

I have the greatest belief in the future of the Belfast theatres. Most people in their hearts love the drama and the old feeling that the theatre is a wicked place is gradually dying away, even among the very religious people. They see that the daily life of actors, now that they are brought more into touch with them, is not what was painted by their forefathers. As a matter of fact, actors and actresses have to lead the quietest and most self-denying life in order to be able for their work nightly.

Mʀ GRIMALDI ᴀꜱ CLOWN.

Price Halfpenny

ILLUMINATING THE ENTRANCE TO OLD GUTTER LANE

English pantomime clown Joseph Grimaldi; his first appearance was at Sadler's Wells in 1781 as an infant dancer, and he regularly performed there until his retirement from the stage in 1828.

THEATRE MUSEUM, V. & A.

The Grand Opera House management made no bones about parading the lavishness of its productions. *Blue Beard* was trumpeted thus:

New and Magnificent Scenery, Designed and Painted by Messrs Brunton, Tritschler, Barry Parker and Kinnimont. Music Composed, Selected and Arranged by Mr J. Dalton Burrows (Musical Director). Charming and Costly Costumes expressly designed by Mrs Dottridge. Wonderful Mechanical Effects and Changes by Mr E. Bax. Elaborate Properties and Appointments by Messrs Robinson and Campbell. The Limelight, Gas Effects, and Illuminations by Mr T.E. Wardell. The Armour by Messrs Kennedy & Co, Birmingham. The Comic Scene invented by Messrs Bertram & Rydon. The New and Popular Songs.

From the beginning of the twentieth century right up to the 1930s, elaborate song books were produced for each Belfast pantomime, giving the words of the popular songs. These were thick volumes, heavily supported by advertising, and a 1905 programme of *Cinderella*, 'invented and produced' by Fred W. Warden and Frederick Mouillot with stage manager J.M. Jones, ran to forty-four pages, with glamorous photographs of the cast. For Fred Warden, pantomimes were a speciality. A souvenir booklet produced for the theatre's fiftieth anniversary in 1945 records:

Although Fred Warden never failed to cater for legitimate drama, his genius really lay in pantomime production. He was, indeed, recognised throughout the British Isles for his outstanding ability in this sphere of entertainment. He had a remarkable flair for selecting the right artistes and for making that harmonious combination of the spectacular and the ingenuous which is the essence of pantomime.

Fred Warden and Frederick Mouillot, both directors of Warden Ltd, 'invented and produced' the 1905 pantomime, *Cinderella*.
GRAND OPERA HOUSE

In the early days the current big stars were imported to Belfast, and 'names' like Carlotta Levy, Mabel Love and Julia Mackay, Tom Foy and George Lashwood took leading roles. One tiny girl, later Margaret Waring, who was to create wonders as wardrobe mistress for the Gang Shows from the 1950s, fell in love at the age of three with the principal boy of a pantomime of the 1920s. Her mother took her to the stage door, and she hit it off immediately with Olive Fox, the principal boy, but was shocked to see the digs the glamorous star was occupying in Amelia Street, and instantly invited her home to stay off the Cliftonville Road, where she was welcome on every return visit. Margaret Waring vividly remembers the 'transformation scenes' of these early pantomimes, which were huge, dramatically staged tableaux. In one scene, for example, the whole stage of the Grand Opera House was transformed into a lady's dressing table: marvellously costumed ladies and acres of gauze gave the impression of mirror and combs, brushes and fans.

Music-hall artistes made their contribution: Will Fyffe, Elsie Prince and the Houston Sisters appeared at the theatre. The 1930s was a particularly golden era. In 1933 *Aladdin* was relayed by the BBC, the first occasion on which a show was broadcast from the stage of the theatre. In 1934 *The Queen of Hearts* attracted large audiences, and it was claimed that this picturesque panto was 'better than ever'. The 1935 version of *Robinson Crusoe* had Elsie Prince, Bunny Doyle, twelve Tiller Girls and a flying ballet. Elsie Prince came back again in 1937 with *Dick Whittington* and the decade ended with a final flourish in 1938 as Wee Georgie Wood took the role of Johnny Green with Hannah Green and the Brothers Egbert in *Babes in the Wood*. The producer responsible for four of these 1930s shows was Fred Tripp, who was to manage and produce the Savoy Players through the Second World War.

The Savoy Players, with their war-limited resources, never attempted to emulate the lavish spectacles of the first half of the century. Instead they put on lighter shows at Christmastime. When the theatre returned to normal, the management invested heavily in pantomimes, making the season a fundamental element of the theatre's annual programme, and continued to adapt to changing fashions and directions. In 1950, Tommy Morgan's *Cinderella* was a huge success, and the pantomime season came to an end with a big social event. The local papers ran advertisements: 'Electors of Ulster! There's only one party to support on 10th February. Tommy Morgan's Farewell Party and CINDERELLA BALL.' The ball was held at the Orpheus Ballroom, dancing (with spot and novelty prizes) was from nine to two, Tommy Morgan provided the cabaret, refreshments were available at moderate prices, and tickets, price 5s. 6d., were on sale at the door with proceeds going to the National Society for the Prevention of Cruelty to Children.

For the expensive *Old King Cole* production of 1954, the management contracted a producer from Anglia Television, Peter Yolland.

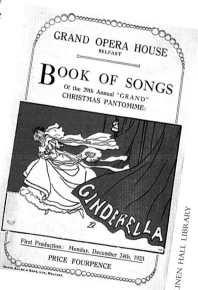

It was during this period that the pantomime was specially popular; it represented for many a magical introduction to the theatre. One small Belfast girl entered a Christmas competition run by that well-loved girls' comic the *School Friend*, for which she drew a traditional picture of carol singers around a lamp-post. To her delight, through the post two tickets came for *Cinderella* at the Grand Opera House. Her brother came with her; the two children were treated royally: best seats, sweets and ice-cream. It was a new world opening up. She instantly fell in love with Buttons (a youthful Des O'Connor), and with the fabulous setting (especially the gorgeous fairy coach), and was fascinated with the trailing silvery streamers that formed part of the set. More important, like many before and after her, because of the pantomime she fell in

Olive Fox, principal boy at pantomimes during the 1920s. A Belfast family, shocked at her theatrical digs in Amelia Street, took her home and were hosts on all her subsequent visits.
MARGARET WARING

1950s programme
LINEN HALL LIBRARY

love with the theatre, and went on, as Maureen Dunn, to make a major contribution to the world of amateur drama in Northern Ireland, as actress and director in Theatre 3 Newtownabbey.

There was no doubt of the commitment of the management of the 1980s to the pantomime. Right from the start, Michael Barnes made no apology for letting the pantomime take a proud place within a quality programme, and although he steered away from the traditional course when he brought big musicals like *Seven Brides for Seven Brothers* for the Christmas season, public demand was such that the pantomime was reinstated after three years. Derek Nicholls unhesitatingly maintained the pantomime season, establishing it even more strongly by making the decision to direct *Aladdin* himself in 1995, following in the footsteps of Fred Warden.

During the 1980s and 1990s the theatre brought a highly successful combination of local stars and names known throughout the British Isles, both from Northern Ireland and beyond. Charlie Daze came, the inimitable Krankies were an immediate hit with the Belfast audience, and Tom O'Connor endeared himself to the city in a very special way. The Grand Opera House had planned to stage *Babes in the Wood* in December 1991, but a devastating pre-Christmas bomb put paid to that. Some members of the company, notably Tom O'Connor, decided to mount a makeshift alternative *Aladdin* in La Mon House Hotel; for all its rough-and-ready nature, the production succeeded in bringing the warmth and colour of a pantomime to Belfast at a time when it needed it. Michael Barnes gave this show his blessing in the programme:

For a reason you will all know, it was impossible for the Grand Opera House to present its scheduled production of *Babes in the Wood*. Naturally, all the staff were very distressed that such a thing should happen, and everyone will understand that the reason was far from our control. Tens of thousands of people, young and old, were inevitably disappointed.

Also disappointed were the stars of this year's Grand Opera House panto – Tom O'Connor, Candy Devine, May McFettridge, John Hewitt among them. They decided to put on a show of their own here at La Mon Hotel. I wish the whole company a great success, and I'm sure they will deserve it.

Let me wish both the company and their audiences a happy New Year. And let me assure you that the Grand Opera House will re-open as soon as possible. And that won't be too long from now.

All the best to everyone.

Michael Barnes

It was not too long before the pantomime was back in the theatre, bringing another generation to see virtually the same shows that their parents had seen. The unchanging nature of the traditional ingredients is part of the magic of the pantomime. There is the outrageous dame

LINEN HALL LIBRARY

May McFettridge, played by John Lenihan, has become a regular favourite at Grand Opera House pantomimes in the 1990s.

DAVID GRAHAM OF HILLSBOROUGH

with false bust and bustle, Technicolor hair and layers of underwear, the principal boy in shiny tights and high heels, the improbably wholesome leading lady and the buffoons; the good fairy and wicked wizard – good always coming on from the right, bad from the sinister left – the good fairy as boring as the wizard is predictable. No pantomime is complete without energetic booing and hissing at the Demon King or his equivalent, or without cries of 'look behind you', or 'oh no it isn't'. Every pantomime must have a slapdash sequence involving a paintbrush or a mixing bowl. The skit with a heavy bag coming down from the ceiling as a little bit of heaven is quite unashamedly brought out again and again. Many pantomimes will have a 'skin' part – a cow or a cat – and every pantomime must have a live orchestra, sentimental songs and a dance with special effects, which return with accepted regularity as the underwater mermaids of one year give way to the skeletons of the next. Just before the finale – a brilliantly costumed set piece – the audience is invited to sing a song; invariably the left side of the house will be asked to

Pantomimes enjoyed a revival after the Second World War, and the 1950 production of *Cinderella* owed its success both to the star attraction, comedian Tony Morgan, and to very successful marketing.

IRELAND'S SATURDAY NIGHT

Frank Carson in *Dick Whittington*, 1982
GRAND OPERA HOUSE

rival the right side of the house in verve and volume, and will compliantly participate.

The jokes do not vary much, either.

Ugly Sister One: I'll just slip my foot into this crystal slipper.
Ugly Sister Two: You couldn't slip your foot into the Crystal Palace.

'Why don't you grow up, stupid.'
'I have grown up stupid'.

The best pantomimes will have, as they have had since Victorian times, topical allusions and local jokes. In Fred Warden's great success *Babes in the Wood*, Mr J.J. Stamford was credited on the programme for adding 'Local and Topical Allusions' to the original script by J.H. Wolfe. In Belfast in the 1980s comic characters were more likely to poke fun at the Cherryvalley accent than the politics of the day, and the old familiar chestnuts of local recognition rarely failed to raise a laugh. Most years the dame will cast aspersions at the snobs sitting in 'the ashtrays' at the side of the stage, and members of the audience will laugh as if they have never heard it before.

Some of the local comics have a special repartee with the audience. May McFettridge, played by John Lenihan, achieved stardom by popular demand when she began to phone Eamonn Holmes when he worked for

Downtown Radio; he/she gained fame, or notoriety, for the outrageous personal appearances that ensued. Described as 'Ulster Housewife and Superstar', the 'sort of woman you might see at the better class of Oxfam shop', she probably (just) avoids offence while sharing her most intimate secrets, giving useful advice about life in general, whether you want it or not, and asking the most outlandish questions. Sometimes, in a Belfast pantomime audience, she will meet a challenge in a heckler with wit, or pick on some poor unfortunate victim, and the audience is treated to a constant bombardment of comic abuse. One of her major talents is her ability to listen, which she uses to great advantage.

Frank Carson gave the Grand Opera House audience his Ulster sense of humour, which had found him a place in the ranks of the top British comics of the day. A master of pinpoint timing, the belly laugh and a famous look of utter stupefaction, not to mention his celebrated catchphrase, 'It's the way I tell them', he brought an unmissable professionalism to the Grand Opera House's first pantomimes after the 1980 reopening.

Another Ulster comedian, Jimmy Cricket, was a great popular favourite. His helpless naïveté and confiding way of bringing in the audience with a gesture of his hand and 'C'mere, there's more', his squeaky clean material and his gentle manners, endeared him to family audiences – and his famous welly boots with *R* and *L* on the toes were a happy addition to the Grand Opera House stage.

Jimmy Cricket's wholesome image endeared him to family audiences in the 1994 production of *Jack and the Beanstalk.*
DAVID GRAHAM OF HILLSBOROUGH

Rose Marie – a popular Dick
Whittington in 1982
GRAND OPERA HOUSE

James Ellis was a different sort of pantomime comedian. A serious actor
of considerable talent, he had acted in the Grand Opera House with the
Group Theatre before he went on to become a household name in the
popular television series *Z Cars*. He continued to act in a wide range of
challenging roles. Perhaps not so challenging was his role as Gertie
Gemmel in *Goldilocks and the Three Bears*, but James Ellis declared it was the
fulfilment of a lifetime's ambition to play a dame.

Of Ulsterwomen who played in the pantomime, Dana was unforgettable
as Snow White, with hair as black, skin as white, lips as red, and smile and
voice as sweet as either the Brothers Grimm or Walt Disney could have
dreamt of. Dana had shot to fame when she emerged as a pretty, unassum-
ing, very young Derry girl to win the Eurovision Song Contest with the
song 'All Kinds of Everything'. She was the archetypical girl-next-door,
who must have found the sudden burst into fame difficult to handle, but
she managed to avoid the famous-for-fifteen-minutes syndrome and
matured into a fine performer, now based in the United States of America,
where she specialises in gospel music.

Rose Marie, the ebullient singer from Newry with a big voice and a big
stage presence, was the perfect foil and complement to Frank Carson when
she played opposite him in *Dick Whittington*; versatile actor John Hewitt
and singer Peter Corry brought their own local interpretations to the

traditionally unchanging role of the villain.

What *has* changed in Grand Opera House pantomimes is the behaviour of the audience. Although the lively participation of the people in the stalls, the circle and the gallery is obligatory for the success of any pantomime, no cast of the 1990s has to put up with the behaviour of the gods on Students' Night on 26 January 1899, as reported by the *Belfast News-Letter*:

> The curtain had scarcely risen when 'the wicked uncle' and 'the two ruffians' received from the gods intellectual numerous tokens of their esteem in the shape of fruit and vegetables, fresh or otherwise. Twice during the evening the students held on their own accord a musical entertainment which was distinctly varied. A gentleman with a silk hat of undoubted antiquity, who wore a white jersey and crimson shawl, upon the back of which in white characters were the words 'Queen's College, Belfast – Medicine' [*sic*]. Doubtless he and his confreres were convinced that laughter was the best physic.

Sometimes it is the cast who get up to mischief. On one New Year's Eve, in a pantomime in which a prominent actor was Scottish, members of the cast and the band created havoc. 'The Bluebells of Scotland' rang out instead of 'Turn Again, Dick Whittington', the monster in the 'Look Behind You' sketch appeared in a kilt doing the Highland Fling, and the musicians created anarchy by improvising Scottish songs and introducing special sound effects at all the wrong times. The audience enjoyed itself immensely.

Quick backstage change by ugly sister Fanny, in *Cinderella* in 1980
BELFAST TELEGRAPH

12
BEYOND THE STAGE DOOR

I N MANY WAYS THE LIFE OF THE THEATRE behind the scenes has changed very little in the past century. The mundane and the magical still cohabit a confined space, and in the best-run theatres the commercial and the creative run side by side. Each professional has his or her own sphere and standards, and yet the only way a theatre can operate properly is when all the individual elements come together in a cohesive unit. The theatre needs the efficiency, vision and astuteness of the administrative staff, the expertise and adeptness of the technical staff, the diplomacy and carefulness of the front-of-house staff. The theatre needs comfortable dressing rooms and attractive bars, and it also needs staff who do not mind cleaning up after one thousand men, women and children in the short space between matinée and evening pantomimes. It needs people who will 'get out' a production in the early hours of Sunday morning. It needs the nimble fingers of a wardrobe mistress and the controlled welcome of an usher greeting five hundred patrons to the stalls in fifteen minutes. There has to be humour behind the scenes but there is intolerance, too, because no theatre can afford the casual or the sloppy.

Photographs shown on pages 156 to 165 were taken behind the scenes during Pola Jones's *Return to the Forbidden Planet* in May 1995 and First Art Productions' *42nd Street* in June 1995
JILL JENNINGS,
CHRISTOPHER HILL PHOTOGRAPHIC

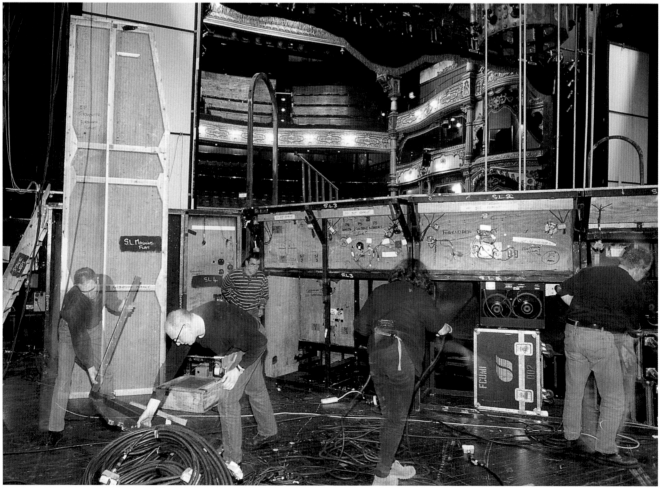

For a major opera production, hundreds of people will present their stage door passes each evening: orchestra and conductor, chorus and principals, wardrobe, make-up and wig staff, stage crew, stage managers, administrators, chaperones for children, the musical expert who, score in hand, works the surtitles machine, the caterer who looks after the corporate sponsors, the members of the St John's Ambulance Brigade. For the first night of the opera some members of the audience will watch with particularly sharp critical faculties. The director and designer will usually leave after the first performance, and the lighting designer will have set up the programme for the run and can leave it in the hands of the technical staff. The repetiteur who played piano at the singing rehearsals has reached the end of his or her contribution as has the choreographer, but they will stay

for the first night. The critics will be seated, usually preferring stalls seats near the aisle in about row J. The conductor's role is primary, and the audience will not be aware of the close contact he has with the singers through the television monitors high behind the proscenium arch. In the wings and on the stairs, in the dark corridors around the back of the stage, up to the fly tower and beyond to the chorus dressing rooms, there is an atmosphere of silent concentration and discipline. When the curtain finally falls, when the last presentations of flowers and kisses have been given and received and the applause comes to an end there is a chance to take a breath, but often this is only a pause before the work starts all over again.

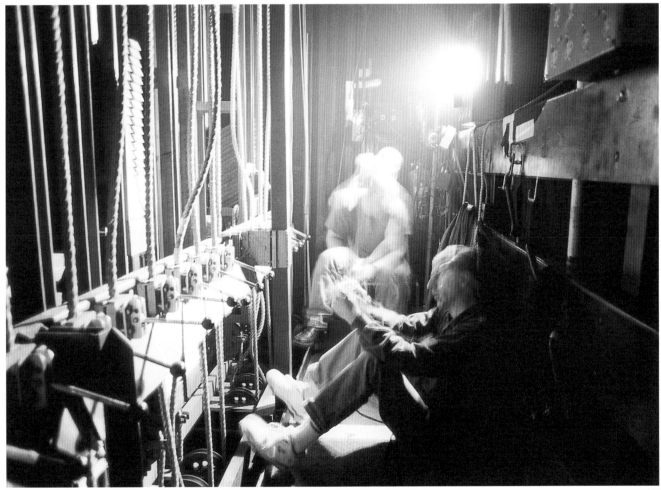

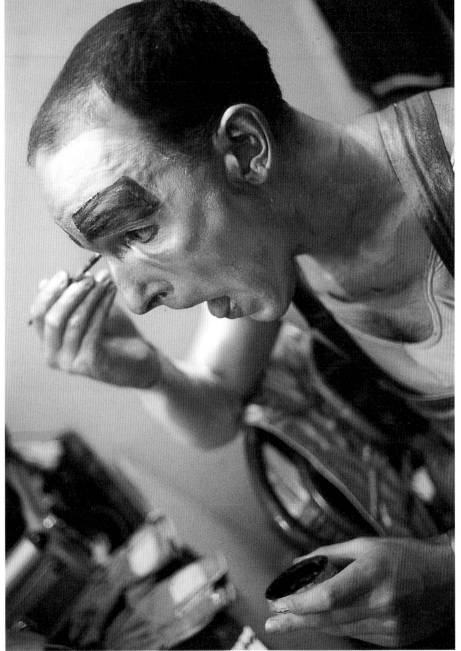

Below:
Derek Nicholls, theatre director
Top right:
Eric Reid, house manager
Bottom right:
John Jordan (left),
technical services manager

CHRISTOPHER HILL

166

ACKNOWLEDGEMENTS

I received much help and support during the preparation of this book. My thanks, in particular, go to Robert Agnew, the Arts Council of Northern Ireland, Harry Auld, Belfast Central Library, Belfast City Council, *Belfast Telegraph*, Jan Bertenshaw, Birmingham Central Library, Blackstaff Press, Sir Charles Brett, Claude Douglas, Beth Duffin, Maureen Dunn, Field Day Theatre Company, Hilary Finch, Charles Fitzgerald, Elizabeth Forbes, Brian, Fergus, Laura and Michael Gallagher, the Gate Theatre, David Graham, John Gray, John Jordan, Marion Kelly, John Knipe, Linen Hall Library, Betty Lowry, the Lyric Theatre, Betty and Cherrie McIlwaine, Eddie McIlwaine, Bob McKeown, Robert McKinstry, Kenneth Montgomery, Monuments and Buildings Record, National Library of Ireland, Derek Nicholls, Opera Northern Ireland, Ivor Preece, Public Record Office of Northern Ireland, Eric Reid, Alan Reynolds, the Scout Association, Margaret Smyth, Gary and Diane Spratt, Carole Stewart, the Theatre Museum at the V. & A., Lesley Townsend, Mary Traynor, Ulster Architectural Heritage Society, the Ulster Folk and Transport Museum, the Ulster Museum, *Ulster News Letter*, Margaret Waring, Wesley Weir, and especially to all those theatre-goers who preserved photographs, programmes and press cuttings throughout the century.

GRATEFUL ACKNOWLEDGEMENT IS ALSO MADE TO:

Appletree Press for permission to quote from *Belfast: The Making of a City* (1988) by J.C. Beckett, *et al*; Blackstaff Press for permission to quote from *Belfast: An Illustrated History* (1982), by Jonathan Bardon; *Frank Matcham, Theatre Architect* (1980), edited by Brian Mercer Walker; *Straight Left: An Autobiography* (1993) by Paddy Devlin; C.E.B. Brett for permission to quote from 'A triumph of plush and gilt', *Country Life* (1980) and *Buildings of Belfast 1700–1914* (revised edition, Friar's Bush Press, 1985); Faber and Faber for permission to quote from *Peter Waring* (1937) by Forrest Reid; Farset Press for permission to quote from *'At Last, a Great Tenor'* (1994) by Leslie Gilmore; Greystone Press for permission to quote from *Fading Lights, Silver Screens: A History of Belfast Cinemas* (1985) by Michael Open; Nick Hern Books for permission to quote from *The Boys* (1994) by Christopher Fitz-Simon; Chatto and Windus for permission to quote from *Beginning* (1989) by Kenneth Branagh; Sceptre Books for permission to quote from *Early Stages* (1987) and *Backward Glances* (1989) by John Gielgud; and Ulster Architectural Heritage Society for permission to quote from *An Introduction to Ulster Architecture* (1975) by Hugh Dixon.

Photographs from Monuments and Buildings Record, Crown copyright: reproduced with the permission of the Controller, Her Majesty's Stationery Office.

SELECT BIBLIOGRAPHY

Arts in Ulster, The, Belfast, 1951

BARDON, Jonathan. *Belfast: An Illustrated History*, Belfast, 1982

BECKETT, J.C., *et al. Belfast: The Making of a City*, Belfast, 1988

BELL, Margaret. *A History of Scouting in Northern Ireland*, Belfast, 1985

BELL, Sam Hanna. *The Theatre in Ulster*, Dublin, 1972

BENN, George. *A History of the Town of Belfast from the Earliest Times to the Close of the Eighteenth Century*, Belfast, 1877

BRANAGH, Kenneth. *Beginning*, London, 1989

BRETT, C.E.B. *Buildings of Belfast 1700–1914*, Belfast, 1985

'A triumph of plush and gilt', *Country Life*, 1980

DEVLIN, Paddy. *Straight Left: An Autobiography*, Belfast, 1993

DIXON, Hugh. *An Introduction to Ulster Architecture*, Belfast, 1975

EVANS, E. Estyn and Brian S. Turner (eds). *Ireland's Eye: The Photographs of Robert Welch*, Belfast, 1977

Festival of Britain 1951 in Northern Ireland, Official Souvenir Handbook, Belfast, 1951

FITZ-SIMON, Christopher. *The Boys*, London, 1994

FROW, Gerald. *'Oh, Yes It Is': A History of Pantomime*, London, 1985

GALLAGHER, Eric. *At Points of Need: The Story of the Belfast Central Mission, 1889–1989*, Belfast, 1989

GIELGUD, John, *Early Stages*, London, 1987

Backward Glances, London, 1989

GILMORE, Leslie. *'At Last, a Great Tenor'*, Belfast, 1994

GUTHRIE, Tyrone. *A Life in the Theatre*, London, 1960

JACKSON, Russell. *Victorian Theatre*, London, 1989

LARMOUR, Paul. *The Architectural Heritage of Malone & Stranmillis*, Belfast, 1991

LAWRENCE, W.J. 'The annals of the old Belfast stage', unpublished manuscript in the Linen Hall Library

MAC LIAMMÓIR, Micheál. *Theatre in Ireland*, Dublin, 1950

MAGUIRE, W.A. *Caught in Time: The Photographs of Alexander Hogg*, Belfast, 1986

O'MALLEY, Conor. *A Poet's Theatre*, Dublin, 1988

OPEN, Michael. *Fading Lights, Silver Screens: A History of Belfast Cinemas*, Antrim,1985

PATTON, Marcus. *Central Belfast, a Historical Gazetteer*, Belfast, 1993

Theatre Museum, The, London, 1987

READER, RALPH. *This is the Gang Show*, Burton-upon-Trent, 1957

REID, Forrest. *Peter Waring*, London, 1937

WALKER, Brian Mercer (ed.). *Frank Matcham, Theatre Architect*, Belfast, 1980

McCandless, R.H., 77
McCann, James, 50, 54, 55
McCarney, Kate, 111, 136
McCarrison, Leslie, 66
McConnell, Sir Robert and Lady, 36
McCowen, Alec, 117
Macdona Company, 49–50
McEwan, Geraldine, 119
McFettridge, May (John Lenihan), 150, 151 (*illus.*), 152–3
McGlade, P. & F., 17
McGreavy, Mary, 64
McGrenera, Seamus, 110
McGuinness, Frank, 118, 142
McIlwaine, Eddie, 79–80
Mackay, Julia, 148
McKee, Marjorie, 132, 134, 136 (*illus.*)
McKellar, Kenneth, 78
McKellen, Ian, 119
McKenna, T.P., 85
McKenna, Virginia, 78
McKeown, Robert, 134, 135, 136 (*illus.*), 137 (*illus.*)
McKinstry, Cherith, 100
McKinstry, Robert, 93, 97–101
McLarnon, Gerard, 77
McManus, Mark, 117
McMaster, Anew, 66
MacMillan, Kenneth, 66
MacNamara, Gerald, 41
Macnaughten, Florence, 128
Macook's Corner, 89
Macready, Sam, 140
Macready, William Charles, 16, 146
Madame Butterfly, 65, 66, 71, 81–2
Madame Conte, 59
Madden, Helen, 140
Magic Flute, The, 98 (*illus.*), 99, 111, 113 (*illus.*)
Magpie, 24, 25–6, 27, 29–30
Maid of the Mountains, The, 48
Majority of One, A, 43
Make or Break, 107
Making History, 118
Man and Superman, 49–50
Man for All Seasons, A, 80
Man Who Came to Dinner, The, 59
Marceau, Marcel, 147
Margaret, Princess, 135
Mariana, 34
Maritana, 128, 136
Marriage of Figaro, The, 110–11
Marshall, Bob, 76
Martin, H. & J., 8, 54, 97–8
Mary, Queen, 20
Mary Rose, 59
Mason, Ronald, 138, 140
Mastersingers, The, 20
Matcham, Frank, 2, 3–7, 16, 31, 94, 101, 103, 117, 124
Maugham, Somerset, 40
Maxwell, D.E.S., 106
May, Eddie, 52
Mayne, Rutherford, 41–2, 43
Mecca Ltd, 89

Melchett, Lord, 95
Melotones, The, 76
Merchant of Venice, The, 19, 52
Mermaid Theatre, 141
Merry Widow, The, 39, 136
Messiah, 12
Metropolitan Ballet, 66
Michel, Keith, 118
Midlands Arts Centre, Birmingham, 124
Midsummer Night's Dream, A, 52, 118
Midsummer Night's Dream, A (ballet), 109
Mignon, 20
Mikado, The, 45 (*illus.*), 53
Miles, Sir Bernard, 141–2
Miller, Arthur, 142
Milligan, Alice, 40
Miricioiu, Nelly, 109
Mr Manhattan, 45
Mr What's-his-name, 50
Mitchell, Ian Priestley, 58
Moffo, Anna, 81
Moiseivitch, Tanya, 69
Montgomery, Field Marshal Sir Bernard, 60
Montgomery, Kenneth, 78, 110–12, 114
Moody Manners Opera Company, 30
Moore, James, 31
Moore, Thomas, 43
Moran, Nuala, 57
Moreau, Jeanne, 80
Morecambe and Wise, 76
Morell, H.H., 8
Morell–Mouillot company, 18
Morgan, Tommy, 76, 149
Morgan, Tony, 151 (*illus.*)
Morrison, Joseph, 134
Morrison, Van, 114–15
Morrow, George, 40, 43
Morrow, Harry, 41
Morrow, Norman, 40, 43
Morshiel, George. *See* Shiels, George
Moscow Balalaika Orchestra, 116
Moths, 38
Mouillot, Frederick, 33, 147–8
Mozart, Wolfgang Amadeus, 20, 111, 114
Much Ado About Nothing, 119
Mulholland, Patricia, 68, 80, 81, 109
Murphy, Irwin, 143 (*illus.*)
Murphy, J.J., 140
music halls, 12
My Fair Lady, 136
My Girl, 18
My Son John, 49

Naming of Cuchullain, The, 42
National Theatre, 77, 85, 118
National Trust, 93–4
Neddy the Lovable Donkey, 53
Neeson, Liam, 106, 140, 141 (*illus.*)
Neill, Michael, 111
Nelson, Dr Havelock, 104
Nesbitt, Edith, 118
Nettles, John, 117
New Grand Opera House and Cirque. *See* Grand Opera House
New Lyric Opera Company, 80

New Way to Pay Old Debts, A, 77
Newpoint Players, 142
Newry Drama Festival, 138
News Letter, 55, 60–1, 108, 138. *See also* Belfast News-Letter
Nicholls, Derek, 124, 145, 150, 166 (*illus.*)
Night Must Fall, 57
No, No, Nanette, 49, 132 (*illus.*)
No Surrender, 41
Nomad, 24, 37, 42
Norman, Betty, 131 (*illus.*), 134, 135, 136 (*illus.*)
Northern Ballet Theatre, 107, 109
Northern Counties railway, 9
Northern Drama League, 138
Northern Dramatic Feis, 56
Northern Ireland Market Surveys, 123
Northern Ireland Office (NIO), 95
Northern Ireland Opera Trust, 89, 90–2, 94, 106
Northern Ireland Tourist Board, 103, 121, 123
Northern Star, 24–5
Northern Whig, 4–5, 24, 31–2, 34–5, 39, 83
reviews, 41
Not for Children, 76
Novello, Ivor, 128
Nutcracker, The, 108

Observe the Sons of Ulster Marching Towards the Somme, 118, 142
O'Callaghan, Liam, 140
O'Callaghan, Maurice, 77
O'Casey, Sean, 49, 142
O'Connell, Dr, 8
O'Connor, Des, 149
O'Connor, Tom, 150
O'D Revels of 1939, 57
O'Dare, Peggy, 58
O'Dea, Jimmy, 57
Oh Kay!, 50
O'Hooligan, Larry, 61 (*illus.*)
Oke, Alan, 109
Oklahoma!, 141
Old King Cole, 73–4, 149
Old Toll House, The, 18
Old Vic, 63–4, 66, 67, 77–8, 134
Oldfield, Mrs, 146
Olivier, Laurence, 68, 74, 85
O'Mara, Kate, 118
O'Neill, Eugene, 142
Only Way, The, 26 (*illus.*), 27 (*illus.*), 38
Open, Michael, 74–5
opera, 20–2, 23, 26–7, 30, 49, 63–6, 70–1, 78, 81–3, 90–2, 98–9, 106, 109–14
amateur, 127–37
Opera House, Buxton, 3
Opera House, Derry, 3, 35
Opera Northern Ireland, 78, 98–9, 110–11, 114
Opera Weeks, 132
Ormiston, Linda, 109
Orpheus ballroom, 149
Osborne Players, 143
O'Shea, Milo, 75, 123 (*illus.*)